Holy Living

Confession

Paul W. Chilcote

Elaine A. Heath
General Editor

HOLY LIVING: CONFESSION

ISBN 9781501877681

Manufactured in the United States of America

19 20 21 22 23 24 25 26 27 28—10 9 8 7 6 5 4 3 2 1

ABINGDON PRESS
Nashville

TABLE OF CONTENTS

For

Isabella Wairimu Gitonga

my granddaughter

a beautiful child of God

1 Timothy 6:11-12

FOREWORD

From the time that individuals began responding to Jesus' call to follow him, they began to learn rhythms of life that would be essential for them to be able to live their lives wholeheartedly for God. Chief among these practices was prayer. Jesus modeled for them how to withdraw from busy service to spend time alone in prayer. He offered prayer verbally in front of them, and when they asked, taught them to pray with the prayer we now call the Lord's Prayer. Following Jesus' ascension, as the disciples waited in Jerusalem "for what the Father had promised," that is, the Holy Spirit, Luke tells us that "all were united in their devotion to prayer" (Acts 1:4, 14). Prayer was foundational and formational, positioning them to receive the Holy Spirit, God's empowering presence that both indwelled and propelled them.

Following that transformative event, in due time they followed the Spirit's leading and bore witness to Jesus "to the end of the earth" (Acts 1:8). Their lives were busy, on the move, teaching, preaching, healing, explaining, encouraging, and confronting the evil and injustice of their society. Yet all of that doing, they knew, had to emanate from a deeply grounded experience of being. Nurturing a loving relationship with God was a central commitment that they, like we, had to learn to practice. Apart from this relationship, their busyness was meaningless. So they and those who followed them in the faith added to the practice of prayer a wide range of spiritual disciplines to strengthen their relationship with God, help them grow in Christlikeness, and fuel them for the work God called them to do.

Some of these practices—things like meditation, simplicity, and fasting—are more inwardly focused. Others are expressed outwardly and corporately—things like confession and worship. And some of the practices can be both, such as prayer. All of them—and there are many—work together to help us achieve lives of balance, anchored securely to Christ and equipped for meaningful engagement with others.

This book is one in a series, each volume focusing on a single practice or discipline. In this volume, Paul Chilcote leads us not just to examine but also to practice the many forms that confession takes. He reminds us that we confess not just our sins but also what we believe about God, God's nature, and God's purposes. I invite you to embrace God's will and God's way for you through confession.

Elaine A. Heath
General Editor

INTRODUCTION

Holy Living: Confession

"Confession," they say, "is good for the soul." But confession is one of those Christian practices to which most people give little thought, at least on a daily basis. Like prayer, in general, a person's need tends to trigger this response, and confession is fundamentally relational. If you have really hurt someone, your desire for reconciliation, one would hope, motivates you to some form of action to make things right. The first step you take is to acknowledge the wound you've caused, and hopefully the restoration of that relationship follows. While the apologetic aspect of confession is an essential component, if our understanding ends there we have a limited understanding at best.

In this study of confession, we will explore the importance of the practice on multiple levels. Together, we will examine and practice the many forms that confession takes. St. Augustine's *Confessions* remains one of the most important devotional classics of the Christian tradition and the concluding words of the opening paragraph provide some hint as to how this practice shapes our lives. "You have made us for yourself," Augustine confesses to God, "and our hearts are restless, until they find rest in you." The practice of confession keeps us on this path in life.

The place I want to start in this exploration of the practice of confession will surprise you. The word *confession* can be used basically in two different ways. We normally think of confession as an acknowledgment of sin or an admission of guilt. The most common use of the term in Christian circles is the phrase "confession of sins." But *confession* can also mean a statement of belief. We not only confess our sins, we also confess our faith. The creeds of the church are an expression of this form of confession. I want to begin with this form of confession because our understanding of what we are doing when we practice confession of our sins finds meaning only in our understanding of who God is, particularly as we know God as Father, Son, and Holy Spirit. So we begin by looking together at our *confession of faith* (not sins) and what we affirm about the nature and purposes of God.

Secondly, I will then turn to the first of three different forms of confession as it relates to our brokenness and our quest for wholeness in life, namely, *individual confession*. "All have sinned and fall short of the glory of God" (Romans 3:23, NRSV). The biblical witness clearly affirms the sinfulness of humanity. This disease, affecting all aspects of life, puts us all at "dis-ease." Our restlessness, to which St. Augustine alluded, reflects this dilemma in which we all stand. The primary questions about all relationships in life revolve around the singular question, what do we do with sin? Individual confession provides an opportunity for us to acknowledge this reality, providing a first step in our healing.

Throughout the course of history (and not just Christian history), *mutual confession* has been another way for people to deal with this problem of brokenness in life. Practicing this form of confession has stood the test of time, from the most ancient processes of reconciliation in the family to the band and class meetings of early Methodism, where devout followers of Jesus shared their failures openly and honestly with one another. Sharing the journey of life in the context of a small group or intimate circle of fellow pilgrims enables us to grow. In the practice of confessing our sins to one another we learn more about ourselves and grow into the holiness—the blessedness—that God intends for us all.

Finally, worship provides one of the most significant contexts for the people of God to confess their sin before God and one another. *Communal confession* in the context of the worshiping community adds yet another dimension to this practice related to growth into holiness. As the great poet, John Donne, observed: "No [one] is an island, entire of itself; every[one] is a piece of the continent, a part of the main." We sin not only as individuals but as a community, and over the centuries the church has found ways to practice confession to realign itself with God's will and way.

This volume on confession in this Holy Living series, then, is designed for individuals and small groups who want not only to learn more about the practice of confession but also how to implement it in their personal and communal lives. It is designed to introduce the practice of confession, suggest ways of living the practice daily, and provide opportunities to grow in a faith community with others who engage with the practice.

CHAPTER ONE
Confession of Faith

When you hear the term *confession*, I presume that it hardly stirs up feelings of eager anticipation. Most of us would just as soon avoid confession at all costs. Like going to the dentist, you know you need to do this, but you put it off as much as possible to some later time. Our reactions actually span the spectrum, I would imagine, from "this is just a meaningless ritual" to "this is just too painful." Interestingly, the term *confession* in Scripture is used almost as much to describe our affirmations about God as it is our acknowledgment of sin. And these two aspects of confession are closely related. If you think about it, your conception of who God is actually determines how you feel about confession. I want to argue that your confession of *faith* necessarily precedes your confession of *sins*. What you believe about God dictates your attitude about the practice of confession. You need to know the One to whom you confess before you are even able to acknowledge fully who you are. If you begin with yourself, you have already lost.

My good friend, Steve Harper, has prayed the following prayer for years. He wrote it initially as an expansion of the Collect for Purity in the *Book of Common Prayer*, which begins "Almighty God, to you all hearts are open, all desires known, and from whom no secrets are hidden." Steve's prayer affords profound insight with regard to our confession of God and our confession of sins.

> You are the One, O God, in whom we are totally
> known and totally loved.
>
> If we were totally known without being totally loved,
> we would keep our distance from you.
> We would hide from you.
> But because we are totally loved, we need not fear
> coming into your presence
> because we know your only desire is to do
> us good.
>
> If we were totally loved without being totally known,
> we could fake it.
> We could be the great pretenders—hypocrites.
> But because we are totally known, we are assured there
> is no aspect of our lives
> of which you are unaware and with regard to
> which you are unwilling to deal.
>
> Realizing we are totally known and totally loved,
> we come to you joyfully and openly,
> confident that you will do exceedingly more
> than we can ask or imagine.
> Thank you. Amen.

If we conceive God as an implacable judge, scrutinizing our every thought, word, and action—the One who only knows us completely—then confession will probably feel like a thousand deaths. On the other hand, if we conceive God as love devoid of righteousness—the One who only loves us fully—then confession can devolve into the indulgence of cheap grace.

It will have little transformative effect on our lives. So we must first be clear about who this God is. Only when we have some clarity about God—the One who fully knows and fully loves—can we enter into this spiritual exercise, the purpose of which is ultimately to restore our relationship with that God and others.

Moreover, if we reverse the priority and make confession first and foremost about us, some hidden obstacles to our own forgiveness and healing may elude us. Human beings are incredibly adept at self-deception. Danger accompanies confession for those who have built their lives on their own goodness, righteousness, or spiritual achievement. Authentic confession depends upon knowledge of God and knowledge of self. Confession must begin in God's goodness, love, and grace, but its value also depends on personal and communal authenticity. In an effort to keep first things first, then, let's begin this study of the practice of confession by looking together at our *confession of faith* (not sins)—what we affirm about the nature and purposes of God.

THE GOD REVEALED IN SCRIPTURE

God reveals God's self to us in a multitude of ways, but no mode of revelation connects with us quite so effectively as the "Word." I use this term in a double sense, meaning both the Word we encounter in the words of Scripture and the Word—Jesus Christ—whom we have come to know. The Word—in both these senses—demonstrates who God is, and in God's self-revelation two interrelated themes immediately seize our attention: love and grace. While the first reflects the essential nature of God and the second describes how Christ manifests both God's essence and purpose, they are closely bound to each other in our understanding of God. We cannot separate grace and love in our minds; God is a God of unbounded love and universal grace.

God puts love into action. The narrative of God's love in Scripture comes to fruition in the story of Jesus. Jesus embodies this divine love both in his incarnation and earthly life and in the redemptive work of the cross and Resurrection. Jesus demonstrates how this love acts differently than the love most people have experienced in life. This love serves, creates safe space for others, washes feet, and ultimately relinquishes self to death for the sake of others. The apostle Paul says that "God proves his love for us in that while we still were sinners Christ died for us" (Romans 5:8, NRSV). Similarly, grace puts flesh on love. From the very beginning of the story of God in Scripture we encounter God's capacity for compassion and grace. But the gracious activity of Jesus, in particular, demonstrates definitively that God's love extends to everyone, excludes none, and manifests God's delight to forgive, re-create, heal, and restore. As Paul explains to the Ephesians, "By grace you have been saved through faith, and this is not your own doing; it is the gift of God" (2:8, NRSV). Love and grace are God's ultimate gifts to the human family.

Unbounded Love. The experiences of life, and even aberrant teachings in the church unfortunately, have twisted and distorted the image of God in the minds of many people. The "Religion Survey" conducted by Baylor University—begun in 2005 and purporting to be the most extensive and sensitive study of religion ever conducted into American religious attitudes, behaviors, and beliefs—reveals some unsettling facts about typical American conceptions of God. In an initial round of findings the researchers discerned the following predominant attitudes about God's character and behavior, describing God as either authoritarian (31.4%), benevolent (23%), critical (16%), or distant (24.4%).[1] In other words, nearly eight out of ten Americans view God as authoritarian, critical, or distant, and only two out of ten view God positively, as good-natured. What a far cry this is from the biblical image of a God who desires everyone to enjoy and celebrate the Creator's love and to participate in it fully. The God of unbounded love remains hidden to so many.

In their work entitled *Unbounded Love*, Clark Pinnock and Robert Brow make an effort to reclaim the vision of a God of unbounded love.[2] Revealed in Scripture, this portrait of the divine comes to fruition, in their view, in the person of Jesus Christ. Three broad themes provide the outline for their image of God. First, God's love extends to all. Second, the primary portrait of God in Scripture is that of a loving parent, not a judge. Third, mutuality and openness characterize the posture of this biblical God.[3] If this is our primary portrait of God, then the ramifications with regard to the practice of confession are rather monumental. God envelops all people—indeed, all creation—in the wooing activity of grace. God surrounds and fills everyone and everything with grace. No one stands outside the possibility of this loving embrace.

For this God, so the argument continues, the primary image that governs all relationships is that of the family, not the courtroom. Moreover, this God is a dynamic and loving triune being who is continually at work, through generosity and sensitivity, to heal and restore. I love the Prayer of Thanksgiving in the United

Methodist Order for Morning Praise and Prayer that affirms, "New every morning is your love, great God of light, and all day long you are working for good in the world."[4] This God delights in the joyful expression of restored relationships in a family of love. Little wonder that Pinnock and Brow conclude: "Understood properly, God is practically irresistible. It is a mystery to us why anyone would reject him who loves them so. Why would anyone reject the One whose very glory consists in everlasting love toward humans?"[5]

John Wesley frequently described God's love as unbounded, unconditional, and unrelenting. Charles Wesley, the lyrical theologian who celebrated "Love Divine, All Loves Excelling," put this vision to flight through his poetic expression of "pure, unbounded love":

> Thy ceaseless unexhausted love,
> unmerited and free,
> delights our evil to remove,
> and help our misery;
>
> Thou waitest to be gracious still;
> thou dost with sinners bear,
> that, saved, we may thy goodness feel,
> and all thy grace declare.
>
> Thy goodness and thy truth to me,
> to every soul abound,
> a vast unfathomable sea,
> where all our thoughts are drowned.
>
> Its streams the whole creation reach,
> so plenteous is the store,
> enough for all, enough for each,
> enough for evermore.[6]

Charles Wesley describes God's love as ceaseless and unexhausted, unmerited and free, faithful and constant, unalterably sure. If you root your practice of confession in this conception of God—the God of unbounded love—then you might actually find yourself looking forward to it. Nowhere is this love experienced more fully than through the gift of God's grace.

Universal Grace. A robust conception of confession also finds deep roots in an engaging vision of God's grace. I find it helpful to view the Christian life as a pilgrimage of "grace upon grace." Our abiding connection with God begins in grace, grows in grace, and finds its ultimate completion in God's grace. Through grace God leads us into a dance of joy, justice, and jubilee in which we seek to radiate God's love, participate in God's reign, and partner in the restoration of all things in the Three-One God. Life in Christ may be properly defined as a grace-filled response to the free gift of God's all sufficient grace. In John Wesley's famous sermon on "Free Grace" he makes three simple but profound points. Grace is a free gift. Grace is offered to all. Grace is present in all. God's grace—the way God manifests love in real time—restores our relationship to God and renews God's own image in our lives. God delights in liberating and restoring the human spirit. We encounter the reality of this grace in two particular divine movements: God's actions of creation and redemption.

I have a very good friend in Britain, David Wilkinson, who is both a theoretical astrophysicist and a theologian. Suffice it to say that all I know about the cosmos I know from David, who currently serves as the Principal of St. John's College at Durham University. According to him, currently we are able to see 100 billion galaxies and each of those galaxies is composed of roughly 100 billion stars.[7] Just let that sink in! This universe is so immense, the "normal" person cannot even do the math. I love the picture that C. S. Lewis masterfully paints of Aslan (his figure of Christ) singing the universe into being in his *Chronicles of Narnia*. Lewis astounds his readers as they witness this grace-filled, creative act. The scene nearly takes your breath away.

> In the darkness something was happening at last. A voice had begun to sing. . . . it seemed to come from all directions at once. . . . Its lower notes were deep enough to be the voice of the earth herself. There were no words. There was hardly even a tone. But it was beyond comparison, the most beautiful noise he had ever heard. It was so beautiful [Digory] could hardly bear it. [8]

Lewis brilliantly captures the Christian vision of God's first great act of grace. God has no "need" for this universe or humanity within it, but it is the nature of love to reach out beyond itself, to overflow in the creation of new relationships of love. This also signals the relational nature of God, something expressed most powerfully in the doctrine of the Trinity. The Incarnation—God taking on human flesh in the person of Jesus of Nazareth—demonstrates this same missional quality. In the fullness of time, God entered human history and reached out to the beloved through Jesus Christ in order to re-create and restore all things in and through him. God's mission of love, we could say, begins in Creation and continues through redemption—God's second great act of grace. The triune God postures in perpetual, grace-filled, outward movement—Father, Son, and Holy Spirit in perennial interaction with one another and the world in a great dance of love.

God's second great act of grace—redemption—consists of two interconnected movements of love. In his sermon "On Working Out Our Own Salvation," John Wesley describes these as two grand heads of doctrine.[9] First, grace pertains to the work of God *for us* in Jesus Christ. Secondly, grace pertains to the work of God *in us* through the power of the Holy Spirit. He calls this first movement of redemptive grace the foundation of the way of salvation. We can think of the second movement as the way in which we experience spiritual transformation through our participation in the love of Christ. If those who seek God do not resist the gracious activity of the Spirit of Christ in their lives, then forgiveness and pardon define the foundation of their lives as the disciples of Jesus. But this is the means by which God's greater goal is achieved. God also seeks to liberate, heal, and restore through the work of grace; grace functions in a therapeutic manner to restore and make us whole.

This dual conception of redemptive grace bears most directly on the way I will be talking about the practice of confession because it points us directly to forgiveness on one hand and restoration or recovery on the other. Through a gracious act of mercy, God does for sinners what they cannot do for themselves. Fallen and broken, the human being relies on God's free act of love in Christ to secure the forgiveness that true reconciliation with God, self, and others requires. As a consequence of God's grace the believer experiences forgiveness as pardon. Scripture teaches that God desires all to receive this gift in their lives. But God's redemptive grace also liberates and heals. To use the technical terms, the redemptive work of Christ through the Spirit is not only forensic (legal), it is also therapeutic (restorative). *Holiness* is a shorthand term for this whole redemptive process by which God restores Christlike love in our lives. The phrase "faith working by love leading to holiness of heart and life" expresses this twofold conception of redemption.

Grace, then, enables the Great Physician to bring wholeness out of brokenness. The goal of the Christian life is not simply the assurance of forgiveness, as important as this is, it is the restoration of the image of Christ in the life of the believer. Athanasius, one of the great saints of the early church, speaking of Christ, once proclaimed: "He, indeed, assumed humanity that we might become God."[10] Charles Wesley both preached and sang that the one thing needful in our lives is the "the restoration of the image of God."[11] The goal toward which all life moves is a sense of overwhelming belonging, inner harmony, and connection—the fullest possible love of God and the fullest possible love of neighbor. This is why God created us and the practice of confession (both of God and of sins) helps move us toward that goal. Jesus not only demonstrates God's intention, he also enables this transformation by the presence of his Spirit in our lives. He serves as our primary exemplar and mentor in this journey of restoration.

The apostle Paul, in his Letter to the Philippians, reminds the community to imitate the Christ of whom they sang in one of the earliest hymns of the church:

> Let the same mind be in you that was in Christ Jesus,
> who, though he was in the form of God,
>   did not regard equality with God
>   as something to be exploited,

but emptied himself,
taking the form of a slave,
being born in human likeness.
And being found in human form,
he humbled himself
and became obedient to the point of death—
even death on a cross.

Therefore God also highly exalted him
and gave him the name
that is above every name,
so that at the name of Jesus
every knee should bend,
in heaven and on earth and under the earth,
and every tongue should confess
that Jesus Christ is Lord,
to the glory of God the Father. (2:5-11, NRSV)

The God we have come to know in Jesus Christ—this God of unbounded love and universal grace—becomes then the subject of our confession of faith.

SCRIPTURAL FOUNDATIONS FOR CONFESSION OF FAITH

Notice the language at the conclusion of this ancient hymn from Philippians. Because of what the Son of God has done, every tongue will "confess that Jesus Christ is Lord." In the Greek language two words, *Iesus Kyrios* (Jesus is Lord), constitute the earliest confession of the Christian faith. In Scripture, confessions of faith both reveal who God is and shape belief in those who read, speak, and hear these words. To use this hymn to illustrate the confession that Jesus Christ is Lord both affirms the God we see in Jesus and begins to shape our lives on the basis of his example. We see God in Jesus, confess that God reigns, and seek to emulate the character of the God we have discovered there.

Words function this way, in fact, in all human interaction. If I say to my wife, "I love you," that is an expression of the love in my heart, but it also functions to build the relationship of love we share. Words both reveal and create meaning, and words about God have the same effect. "If you confess with your lips that Jesus is Lord and believe in your heart that God raised him from the dead, you will be saved" (Romans 10:9, NRSV), Paul explained to the followers of Jesus in Rome. "For it is with your heart that you believe and are justified, and it is with your mouth that you profess your faith and are saved" (Romans 10:10, NIV). It should not surprise us that the apostle places such a strong emphasis on the power of words. He had experienced the potency of God's words in his own life. He understood that words shape us and give meaning to our lives.

According to Amanda Drury, testimony and confession go beyond describing something from the past or something you believe. Confession of faith and testimony change us, and when we fail to put our experience of God or beliefs about God into words, we run the risk of stunting our faith. These practices form your present and future identity. Drury describes one's testimony of faith as an essential practice for Christian spiritual formation, especially for those who are in the process of developing their identity.[12] Saying is believing. Apply this lesson to the experience of Martha of Bethany in relation to her conversation with Jesus at the funeral of her brother, Lazarus. Martha speaks out of the depth of her grief:

> Martha said to Jesus, "Lord, if you had been here, my brother would not have died. But even now I know that God will give you whatever you ask

> of him." Jesus said to her, "Your brother will rise again." Martha said to him, "I know that he will rise again in the resurrection on the last day." Jesus said to her, "I am the resurrection and the life. Those who believe in me, even though they die, will live, and everyone who lives and believes in me will never die. Do you believe this?" She said to him, "Yes, Lord, I believe that you are the Messiah, the Son of God, the one coming into the world." (John 11:21-27, NRSV)

In speaking these words, Martha articulated the belief that had captured her life and would continue to shape her as a faithful disciple of Jesus. This confession defined her.

There are many other instances in Scripture where confession connotes an affirmation of faith as opposed to an acknowledgment of sin. All these statements in the New Testament revolve around the lordship of Jesus and the gospel. In writing to the Corinthian community, Paul applauds the church for its "obedience to the confession of the gospel of Christ" (2 Corinthians 9:13, NRSV). The writer to the Hebrews admonishes his readers to "hold fast to our confession" (Hebrews 4:14, NRSV). In John's Gospel specific reference is made to the way in which the confession of Jesus as the Messiah could put the believer at risk, namely, the possibility of expulsion from the synagogue (9:22; 12:42). One's confession of faith, in other words, entails a potential cost.

But the most dramatic use of this language comes in the Epistles of John in which confession refers explicitly to an affirmation of the Incarnation and infers an intimate connection with God. "By this you know the Spirit of God: every spirit that confesses that Jesus Christ has come in the flesh is from God, and every spirit that does not confess Jesus is not from God. . . . By this we know that we abide in him and he in us, because he has given us of his Spirit" (1 John 4:2-3, 13, NRSV; see also 2 John 7). Later in the same chapter, John again equates this confession with intimate connection to God. "And we have seen and do testify that the Father has sent his Son as the Savior of the world. God abides in those who confess that Jesus is the Son of God, and they abide in God. So we have known and believe the love that God has for us" (1 John 4:14-16, NRSV). The confession of faith, in other words, demonstrates knowledge of and connection with the God of unbounded love. Those who have embraced and confessed Christ both know and believe the ultimate reality in life. They have truly come to themselves and celebrate their true identity as the children of God.

HISTORIC CONFESSIONS OF FAITH

Irenaeus of Lyons developed one of the first Christian confessions of faith or creeds outside the canon of the New Testament. By this point in time, creeds—or Rules of Faith—helped to safeguard the apostolic witness to the God of love and grace. Undoubtedly, you will recognize some of the common features of Christian creeds in this second-century formulation:

> For the Church, though dispersed throughout the whole world, even to the ends of the earth, has received from the apostles and their disciples this faith: in one God, the Father Almighty, who made the heaven and the earth and the seas and all the things that are in them; and in one Christ Jesus, the Son of God, who became incarnate for our salvation; and in the Holy Spirit, who proclaimed through the prophets

> the dispensations and the advents, and the birth from a virgin, and the passion, and the resurrection from the dead, and the incarnate ascension into heaven of the beloved Christ Jesus, our Lord, and His future manifestation from heaven in the glory of the Father *to sum up all things* and to raise up anew all flesh of the whole human race.[13]

Note the Trinitarian nature of this affirmation and its focus on creation and redemption, those twin graces that reflect the purposes of God. The creedal statement recites God's mighty acts of salvation. In his magisterial one-volume systematic theology entitled *Doxology*, Geoffrey Wainwright observes:

> Both thanksgiving to God and proclamation before the world are confession of faith (*exhomologein* can also mean 'confess'): they declare our belief that we are included in the scope of God's action and have been touched by it. It is not surprising that creeds also, as confessions of faith, should include some narrative recital of the mighty acts of God on behalf of humanity.[14]

Like Irenaeus's primitive confession of faith, the Apostles' Creed does this as well.

This creed stands out, no doubt, as one of the most recognizable and well-known statements of the Christian faith, embraced by a large number of Christian communions around the world. The components of this statement emerged out of the baptismal practice of the Roman church in which candidates for Christian discipleship were interrogated as part of the baptismal ritual. Some traditions today, like that of The United Methodist Church, have reintroduced an interrogative form of the creed into worship.

Do you believe in God the Father?
I believe in God, the Father Almighty,
creator of heaven and earth.

Do you believe in Jesus Christ?
I believe in Jesus Christ, his only Son, our Lord,
[who was conceived by the Holy Spirit,
born of the Virgin Mary,
suffered under Pontius Pilate,
was crucified, died, and was buried;
he descended to the dead.
On the third day he rose again;
he ascended into heaven,
is seated at the right hand of the Father,
and will come again to judge the living and the dead.]

Do you believe in the Holy Spirit?
I believe in the Holy Spirit,
[the holy catholic church,
the communion of saints,
the forgiveness of sins,
the resurrection of the body,
and the life everlasting.][15]

Scripture provides the language for many of the creedal statements such as this one. Phrases in Paul's writings, such as 1 Corinthians 8:6, seem to quote liturgical material and bear striking resemblance to the first and second articles of the Apostles' Creed: "For us there is one God, the Father, from whom are all things and for whom we exist, and one Lord, Jesus Christ, through whom are all things and through whom we exist" (NRSV). We also find the early *kerygma* of the church (the proclamation of the death and resurrection of Jesus) echoed in the article related to Jesus' redemptive work. Wainwright points out "an obvious affinity between our creeds and some of the New

Testament texts which modern scholars have designated as 'hymns.'"[16] He illustrates this connection with 1 Timothy 3:16 (HCSB):

> He was manifested in the flesh,
> vindicated in the Spirit,
> seen by angels,
> preached among the nations,
> believed on in the world,
> taken up in glory.

"At its most characteristic, the Christian hymn," maintains Wainwright, "may perhaps be considered as a sung confession of faith."[17] Certainly many, if not most, Christians learn the faith initially by singing it. Sacred songs and hymns function as mini catechisms that transmit the central concerns of the Christian way. One of the most ancient Christian hymns illustrates this beautifully.

The *Te Deum*—one of the most significant lyrical confessions of faith in Christian history—reflects the grandeur of God. While the origins of this canticle remain shrouded in mystery, some scholars attribute this majestic act of praise to the fourth-century Serbian bishop, Niceta of Remesiana. Read and ponder each section of this great confession of faith.

> You are God: we praise you;
> You are the Lord: we acclaim you;
> You are the eternal Father:
> All creation worships you.
>
> To you all angels, all the powers of heaven,
> Cherubim and Seraphim, sing in endless praise:
>   Holy, holy, holy Lord, God of power and might,
>   heaven and earth are full of your glory.

The glorious company of apostles praise you.
The noble fellowship of prophets praise you.
The white-robed army of martyrs praise you.
Throughout the world the holy Church acclaims you;
  Father, of majesty unbounded,
  your true and only Son, worthy of all worship,
  and the Holy Spirit, advocate and guide.

You, Christ, are the king of glory,
the eternal Son of the Father.
When you became man to set us free
you did not shun the Virgin's womb.

You overcame the sting of death
and opened the kingdom of heaven to all believers.
You are seated at God's right hand in glory.
We believe that you will come and be our judge.

Come then, Lord, and help your people,
bought with the price of your own blood,
and bring us with your saints
to glory everlasting.[18]

Following the 16th World Methodist Conference in Singapore in 1991, the Executive Committee established a special Work Group for the task of developing a substantive theological paper on the question of diversity and pluralism, focusing in particular on the Wesleyan perspective. The committee tasked with this responsibility produced a document entitled "Wesleyan Essentials of the Christian Faith." This statement, including affirmations about Wesleyan beliefs, service, common life, worship, and witness, was adopted by the World Methodist Conference meeting in Rio de Janeiro in 1996. Dr. Ned Dewire who chaired this process invited me to prepare a "liturgical expression" of the approved essentials statement. This litany provides yet another example of a confession of faith, specifically from a Wesleyan tradition.

We confess the Christian faith,
once delivered to the saints:
shaped by the Holy Scriptures,
guided by the apostolic teaching,
and rooted in the grace of God,
which is ever transforming our lives
and renewing our minds in the image of Christ.

SPIRIT OF FAITH COME DOWN,
REVEAL THE THINGS OF GOD.

We worship and give our allegiance to the Triune God;
gracious to create and mighty to redeem,
ever ready to comfort, lead, and guide,
ever present to us in the means of grace,
uniting us in Baptism and nourishing us in
the Supper of the Lord,
who calls us in our worship to become
sacred instruments of justice and peace,
to love and serve others
with a faith that makes us dance and sing.

O FOR A THOUSAND TONGUES TO SING
MY GREAT REDEEMER'S PRAISE.

We bear witness to Jesus Christ in the world
through word, deed, and sign, earnestly seeking
to proclaim God's will for the salvation
of all humankind,
to embody God's love through acts
of justice, peace, mercy, and healing,
and to celebrate God's reign here and now,
even as we anticipate the time when
God's rule
will have full sway throughout the world.

JESUS, THOU ART ALL COMPASSION,
PURE, UNBOUNDED LOVE THOU ART.

We will strive with God through the power of the
Holy Spirit
for a common heart and life, binding all believers
together;
and knowing that the love we share in Christ
is stronger than our conflicts,
broader than our opinions,
and deeper than the wounds
we inflict on one another,
we commit ourselves to the solidarity
of nurture, outreach, and witness,
remembering our gospel commitment
to love our neighbors
whoever and wherever they may be.

HE BIDS US BUILD EACH OTHER UP,
AND GATHERED INTO ONE,
TO OUR HIGH CALLING'S GLORIOUS HOPE, WE HAND
IN HAND GO ON.

We will work together in God's name,
believing that our commitment comes to life in
our actions:
Like Christ, we seek to serve, rather than
to be served,
and to be filled with the energy of love.
With God's help we will express this love through
our sensitivity to context and culture,
our compassion for the last and the least,
and our commitment to a holiness of heart
and life
that refuses to separate conversion and
justice,
piety and mercy, faith and love.

TO SERVE THE PRESENT AGE,
MY CALLING TO FULFILL,
O MAY IT ALL MY POWERS ENGAGE TO DO
MY MASTER'S WILL![19]

These historic creeds and this lyrical affirmation of faith demonstrate how all confessions of faith are intended to function. Our first response to God is an acknowledgment of the One we worship. In adoration we offer love back to God because we have been loved. We love God for God's self, for God's very being, for God's constancy, for God's radiant joy and everlasting love. We adore the Creator for the magnificent universe that God has sung into existence out of nothing. We adore the Son for all he has done for us to bring us back to our true selves. We adore the Spirit for the transforming power of God's presence in our lives still. Confessing our faith enables us to entrust our lives to God and places us in the appropriate posture of a beloved child of God.

Confession of faith leads quite naturally to confession of sins. We make confession within the embrace of the God who first loved us. In speaking about the Sacrament of Reconciliation, Pope Francis affords this beautiful image from the Orthodox heritage. "I have always been moved by the gesture in the tradition of the Eastern churches," he observes, "where the confessor welcomes the penitent by putting his stole over the penitent's head and an arm around his shoulder, as if embracing him. It is the physical representation of acceptance and mercy."[20] The starting point for all confession is the realization that God loves us—God loves you—unconditionally. We do not confess our sins in the hope that God will then love us. God already loves you and always will. We confess our sins to embrace the God we have come to know through Jesus in the power of the Spirit. We confess our sins to grow into our baptismal identity as God's beloved children.

PRACTICING CONFESSION OF FAITH

There are many ways for you to practice confession of faith as individuals and in a group. Here are several suggestions that can help root you in a robust understanding of who God is and what you and the church affirm about the Father, Son, and Holy Spirit.

Jesus Is Lord Breath Prayer. Breath prayer predates the Christian faith, but disciples of Jesus have been practicing it for generations. When God created human beings, the Scriptures tell us that God breathed into us the breath of life. Breath means life. If you have ever been in a situation in which it was difficult to breathe, you know how crucial breath is to life. So aligning prayer with something so basic to life can be profound.

Our breathing consists of two basic actions. We exhale and we inhale. One way to turn this breathing process into prayer is to think about the act of exhaling as emptying. When you exhale, if you think about those things in your life that you want to get rid of, this can be a very cleansing activity. After you have expelled those negative, dark aspects of brokenness, you are then prepared to open yourself to God's goodness. Think of inhaling as filling. So in the act of inhaling, draw in all that goodness God offers to you as a gift: love, joy, peace. With each exhale, associate those negative aspects of your life with a simple phrase like "empty me fully." Simply say those words in your mind and spirit as you exhale. Then, as you inhale, associate the gifts with which God seeks to fill you with the confession, "Jesus is Lord." In your mind and spirit say these words as you take in this breath of life.

"Empty me fully." "Jesus is Lord." Find a place where you can be quiet as you practice this exercise. Sit and relax your body, mind, and spirit. Begin to think about your breathing. Focus your attention there and center yourself in the simple act of breathing out and breathing in. Try focusing on your breathing in this way for a minute or two, and then silently incorporate these phrases into the rhythm of your breathing. "Empty me fully." "Jesus is Lord." This would be a great way to start the day or finish the day. As stress begins to rise in the course of the day, it might be a helpful way to reduce that stress and find greater peace in the rhythms of the day. Make an effort to engage in this breath prayer each day for a week or more, and see how this confession of faith affects your life, your life with God, and your life with others.

Meditation on Creeds. As we have seen, the early creed, "Jesus is Lord," was one of the earliest confessions of faith. But we have also examined more complex statements of faith like the Apostles' Creed. Another way to practice confession of faith is to meditate on a statement like this one, and there are a couple general ways you can do this.

- Memorize the Creed. Perhaps this is something you have already done with regard to the Apostles' Creed. But what about other statements or confessions of faith? Pick a creed that "speaks" to you, either provided here or that you find elsewhere. Spend time each day simply reading through the creed slowly and meaningfully. At the end of a week see if you actually have not memorized it unconsciously. Some of the words will flow undoubtedly without your even having to think about them. Other words or phrases might elude you. It might be worth asking the question, why is it easy for me to remember this part but difficult to retain another aspect of the creed? Ponder this, but press on, then, to memorize the confession.

- Ponder a Confession of Faith. Ponder each phrase of the statement individually and attempt to plumb the depths of the meaning of the words. To use the Apostles' Creed as an example, this statement of faith contains sixteen phrases. Set aside sixteen days and meditate on one phrase each day. In just over two weeks you will have immersed yourself in one of the most historic confessions of the Christian faith, and your spirit will be shaped by these historic words.

To help with regard to your meditation I suggest that you ask three simple questions of each phrase of the creed. (1) What does each of the words in this phrase mean? (2) What do these words mean to and for me? (3) How am I called to live my life in relation to these words? Pondering anything really does revolve around the questions we ask much more than the answers we give. Those questions stir up our reflection and actually draw us into the reality upon which we meditate. In a brief prayer invite God to guide you in your meditation and then, as you complete your meditation, in a closing prayer express your appreciation to God for the insight you have gained and the deeper relationship you now have.

Martin Luther's Four-Stranded Garland. When his barber and friend, Peter Beskendorf, asked him how to pray, Martin Luther responded with a letter that he later published as a little tract entitled *A Simple Way to*

Pray. Thinking about his friend's profession, he developed this simple model for prayer, emphasizing the focus, discipline, and concentration it requires. This process consists of four movements or strands that Luther wove together to produce what he called a "four-stranded garland." First, he recommended that you reflect upon a text with an open heart, looking for the specific instruction the Lord may have for you. Second, give thanks to God with a grateful heart for all the possibilities laid out before you in the subject of your reflection. Third, ask the Holy Spirit to reveal whatever sins you may need to confess relative to the topic. Fourth, pray about how the Lord wants you to live out your discoveries in your daily life.

This simple pattern of reflection and prayer provides another way to practice confession of faith in a more structured way. Luther actually suggested using this model of prayer in reflection on the Lord's Prayer, the Ten Commandments, and the Apostles' Creed. He used the First Commandment to illustrate the practice.

I think of each commandment as, first, instruction, which is really what it is intended to be, and consider what the Lord God demands of me so earnestly. Second, I turn it into a thanksgiving; third, a confession; and fourth, a prayer. I do so in thoughts or words such as these:

> *[Instruction].* Here I earnestly consider that God expects and teaches me to trust him sincerely in all things and that it is his most earnest purpose to be my God. I must think of him in this way at the risk of losing eternal salvation. My heart must not build upon anything else or trust in any other thing, be it wealth, prestige, wisdom, might, piety, or anything else.

[Thanksgiving]. Second, I give thanks for his infinite compassion by which he has come to me in such a fatherly way and, unasked, unbidden, and unmerited, has offered to be my God, to care for me, and to be my comfort, guardian, help, and strength in every time of need. We poor mortals have sought so many gods and would have to seek them still if he did not enable us to hear him openly tell us in our own language that he intends to be our God. How could we ever—in all eternity—thank him enough!

[Confession]. Third, I confess and acknowledge my great sin and ingratitude for having so shamefully despised such sublime teachings and such a precious gift throughout my whole life, and for having fearfully provoked his wrath by countless acts of idolatry. I repent of these and ask for his grace.

[Prayer]. Fourth, I pray and say: "O my God and Lord, help me by thy grace to learn and understand thy commandments more fully every day and to live by them in sincere confidence. Preserve my heart so that I shall never again become forgetful and ungrateful, that I may never seek after other gods or other consolation on earth or in any creature, but cling truly and solely to thee, my only God. Amen, dear Lord God and Father. Amen."[21]

After you have prayed the four-strand garland, replicate this model in your practice of confession. Reflect or meditate on any confession of faith, like the Apostles' Creed, using this structured pattern. Luther most certainly viewed this model for prayer as an aid to the spiritual life. He has gifted you with a helpful structure for your reflection, not a rigid formula to follow. Open your heart to the presence of the Holy Spirit as you engage in this practice and follow the Spirit's lead.

Create Your Own Creed. Another way to practice confession of faith is to create your own, personal creed or credo. What, in fact, do you believe? Who is God? What are the most important aspects of God's character? Who are you? Who does God call you to be and what does God call you to do? Try to put your affirmations about God, the church, or your relation to God and your place in the world into your own words. Stating propositions in answer to these kinds of questions is extremely difficult but well worth the effort. It might be helpful to restrict yourself to a word limit or a set number of sentences. The more clear, concise, and simple you are, the better. Those ideas or concerns that come quickly to mind as you address the question about what you believe tell you something about the core of your faith. What surfaces first in your mind? Which propositions do you find easier to articulate? Conversely, where do you struggle to figure out exactly what you believe? What is really clear and what remains ambiguous or uncertain?

After you have created your own creed, spend some time with it. Reflect on it daily for a week. Ask yourself the more deeply personal questions like, How do these beliefs affect how I live? Does my life reflect these beliefs? Do I "practice what I preach"? Also, this practice of confession of faith bears repeating. Try doing this again six months later without reviewing your original creed. Compare the two. How has your creed changed? What remains consistent? What new elements have surfaced? Why?

Questions for Personal Reflection and Group Discussion

1. What is your perspective on and experience with confession?

2. The author proposes a broader definition for the practice of confession than simply asking for forgiveness and trying to make amends. How does the author's expanded definition resonate or challenge your understanding of confession?

3. The author argues that Scripture reveals God to be a God of unbounded love and universal grace.
   - What scriptural references and personal experiences reveal a God of unbounded love in your life and in the world?
   - What scriptural references and personal experiences reveal a God of universal grace in your life and in the world? What confessions of faith have you encountered in Scripture? How have they taught you about God?

4. What confessions of faith does your congregation use in worship? Find them (perhaps in a hymnal or other worship resource) and read them.

5. Go back to page 31 and review the section "Practicing Confession of Faith." If you have not already done so, identify one way to practice your own confession of faith.

CHAPTER 2
Individual Confession

Dietrich Bonhoeffer begins a discussion of "confession and communion" in his poignant volume on *Life Together* with these compelling statements:

> He who is alone with his sin is utterly alone. . . . Pious fellowship permits no one to be a sinner. So everybody must conceal his sin from himself and from the fellowship. We dare not be sinners. Many Christians are unthinkably horrified when a real sinner is suddenly discovered among the righteous. So we remain alone with our sin, living in lies and hypocrisy. The fact is that we *are* sinners![1]

The apostle Paul, in his Letter to the Romans, puts it rather bluntly: "all have sinned and fall short of the glory of God" (3:23, NRSV). Scripture bears witness to the fact that sin is total, radical, and universal. Its twin pillars are pride and self-deception. Sin has a corrosive effect; it breaks down relationships. It alienates us from God, from one another, and ultimately from our very selves. It creates walls, destroys hope, creates fear, and robs us of joy. Sin leads to death. Like an unrelenting burden, it clings to us.

Charles Wesley described the debilitating effects of sin in one of his most potent hymns on redemption:

Weary of this war within,
  Weary of this endless strife,
Weary of ourselves and sin,
  Weary of a wretched life;

Burdened with a world of grief,
  Burdened with our sinful load,
Burdened with this unbelief,
  Burdened with the wrath of God.[2]

He could easily have drawn his imagery from Anselm's timeless declaration: "You have not yet considered how heavy the weight of sin is."[3] But God seeks to redeem this situation through an amazing act of love. When Jesus befriends the sinner and those who are wearied and burdened open their hearts to a God of grace, that friendship liberates, heals, and restores. The first step in every Twelve-Step recovery program is the acknowledgment of brokenness. Healing and recovery begin with this honest admission. Our sin—our brokenness—mandates confession.

If the goal of the Christian life is reconciliation and wholeness, then confession stands at the very beginning of this restorative journey and must accompany us each step of the way. We wash our hands frequently—we could even say continually—to prevent illness and the spread of disease. In the same way that washing our hands guards our health, confessing our sins opens us to the cleansing activity of the Holy Spirit. Through the act of confessing we empty ourselves of life-denying words and actions so as to be filled with the life-giving power of love. Confession grounds our lives in the love of God and enables us to be the channels of love to others. Confession heals us. In a General Audience of February 19, 2014, Pope

Francis used this kind of language to describe the confession of sins:

> The Sacrament of Reconciliation is a Sacrament of healing. When I go to confession, it is in order to be healed, to heal my soul, to heal my heart and to be healed of some wrongdoing. The biblical icon which best expresses them in their deep bond is the episode of the forgiving and healing of the paralytic, where the Lord Jesus is revealed at the same time as the physician of souls and of bodies (cf. Mk 2:1-12; Mt 9:1-8; Lk 5:17-26).[4]

SCRIPTURAL FOUNDATIONS FOR INDIVIDUAL CONFESSION

The scriptural foundations for individual confession provide a full range of metaphors and images related to this important spiritual practice. The language of confession pervades the Psalms: a couple of allusions must suffice. "I confess my iniquity; / I am sorry for my sin" (38:18, NRSV). Psalm 32:5 not only describes the human need but celebrates the divine action:

> Then I acknowledged my sin to you,
>   and I did not hide my iniquity;
> I said, "I will confess my transgressions to the LORD,"
>   and you forgave the guilt of my sin. (NRSV)

In the New Testament, John provides one of the most powerful statements about confession and forgiveness:

> If we say that we have fellowship with him while we are walking in darkness, we lie and do not do what is true; but if we walk in the light as he himself is in the light, we have fellowship with one another, and the blood of Jesus his Son cleanses us from all sin. If we

say that we have no sin, we deceive ourselves, and the truth is not in us. If we confess our sins, he who is faithful and just will forgive us our sins and cleanse us from all unrighteousness. (1 John 1:6-9, NRSV)

But nowhere in Scripture are repentance and confession more poignantly portrayed than in the longest of Jesus' parables recorded in Luke's Gospel (15:11-32), a narrative about a father and two sons.[5]

You know the story well. A young son has requested his inheritance, squandered all he has, and finds himself miserable, alone, starving, dying, lost. Stripped of dignity, value, and identity, the critical turning point in the story comes with these important words, "But when he came to himself. . . ." John Wesley is the only theologian I have ever found to define repentance as "true self-understanding." And I am certain he takes his definition from Jesus' parable. The prodigal "came to himself." In the depth of his despair, he remembered who he was and to whom he belonged. But that rediscovery was a two-edged sword.

On the one hand, he understood too well who he was in that moment. He realized how far he had strayed. He was overcome with a sense of guilt and shame. He understood exactly what it meant to lose the dignity of his sonship. And that discovery—that self-revelation—broke his heart. But on the other hand, he came to himself in the sense of acknowledging the one to whom he belonged, realizing that nothing could ever strip him of his primary and eternal identity. He would always be his father's son, regardless. His repentance was an act of contrition and a reclamation of identity.

And so, the prodigal begins the long journey home, with his well-rehearsed greeting of sincere humility and remorse—of hope. "Father, I have sinned against heaven and before you; I am no longer worthy to be called your son" (verses 18 and 21, NRSV). "This is the son's confession compacted into a single sentence," observes Jim Forest in his classic study of the doorway to forgiveness. "It is the essence of any confession."[6] What he longed for more than anything else in his life was the face of the one he loved. Nothing could have prepared him for what he experienced in his father's arms just in sight of his home. Father Maurizio Compiani, in his catechetical materials on confession, concludes: "Within this reborn relationship the father's gifts to his son only amplify his love, which has never lessened, and reestablish the signs of filial dignity the son thought he had lost. Just like Jesus with the paralytic of Capernaum ('Child, your sins are forgiven,' Mk 2:5), this father also gives back to his son his true identity."[7] The portrait of repentance, confession, and responding love captures the essence of Henri Nouwen's insight: being the beloved expresses the core truth of our existence. "The Father is always looking for me with outstretched arms," he professes, "to receive me back and whisper again in my ear: 'You are my Beloved.'"[8]

Richard Foster's commentary on this parable of forgiveness is worth quoting at length:

> Not only is it true that "we love, because he first loved us," but we are enabled to make confession only and especially because he first loved us (1 John 4:19). The evidence of mercy and grace sparks a contrite heart and allows confession to flow. We are drawn to him as Hosea tells us, "with cords of compassion, with the bands of love" (Hos. 11:4). We come with hopeful hearts, for the One we are coming to waits for us like

> the father of the prodigal who saw his son when he was still a great way off and in compassion ran and embraced him and welcomed him back (Luke 15:20). His greatest delight is to forgive. He calls his light-filled creatures of heaven into celebration whenever one person makes confession.[9]

Repentance marks our turning to God and our return to our true selves. Forgiveness is a mystery; confession is the key that unlocks the door.

CLASSIC ELEMENTS OF INDIVIDUAL CONFESSION

The various Christian traditions approach the practice of confession differently and use language about it that is distinctive to their practice. Most Protestants understand the term *confession* rather generically, as one important element of a process by which people seek God's and other's forgiveness. Technical terms such as Penance, the Sacrament of Penance and Reconciliation, or the Rite of Reconciliation all refer to more formalized ritual practices, primarily of the Roman Catholic and Orthodox traditions, which view confession as one of seven sacraments. While Protestants eventually shifted their thinking about its character as a sacrament, Martin Luther held on to the penitential rites much longer than most. Whether understood generically or sacramentally, however, most traditions would agree with the Orthodox theologian Alexander Schmemann in identifying three key relationships that require confession: relationship to God, relationship to others, and relationship to one's self.[10] In his *Small Catechism* Martin Luther delineated two parts of confession: the actual confession of sins and the reception of absolution. He viewed the equal importance of both in the process of reconciliation. Beyond this, many recognize at least five fundamental movements in the practice of individual confession: examination of conscience, contrition, confession, satisfaction, and absolution. No matter what the approach to confession—spontaneous or ritualized—each of these plays a significant role in our healing and quest for wholeness in life.

Examination of Conscience. All confession begins with a close scrutiny of our interior lives. In that central space of our being—the "citadel of the heart" as Howard Thurman described it—we nurture all our hopes and fears, hatreds and loves. Our conscience resides there. Thomas à Kempis, author of *The Imitation of Christ*, made conscience one of the central pillars of his spirituality. At one point, his discussion of the conscience evoked this prayer: "I offer you all my sins and offences, O Lord, on the altar of your mercy. . . . Consume them all with the fire of your love and wash out all the stains of my sins. Cleanse my conscience from all offences and restore your grace to me, which I lost by sin. Forgive all my offences and receive me mercifully with the kiss of peace!"[11] He made it a regular practice to examine his own conscience daily in an effort to orient all his actions toward the good. Many of the spiritual writers who discuss examination of conscience quote this incisive statement of Douglas Steere: "This is a time where a soul comes under the gaze of God and where in His silent and loving Presence this soul is pierced to the quick and becomes conscious of the things that must be forgiven and put right before it can continue to love the One whose care has been so constant."[12]

Marjorie Thompson discusses the examination of conscience in *Soul Feast: An Invitation to the Christian Spiritual Life*. Her insight merits close attention particularly because of its practical value. "Confession," she writes, "unlocks a process of spiritual healing, opening us to forgiveness, cleansing, reconciliation, and renewal. But we cannot confess our sins unless we know what they are. This is where the art of self-examination comes into play."[13] But self-examination is hard work; we don't always like what we see in the mirror. We have an amazing ability to cover up our sins; our capacity for self-deception even clouds our self-understanding. Thompson likens examination of conscience to the fourth step of popular Twelve-Step recovery programs, namely, the need to "make a fearless and searching moral inventory of ourselves."[14] Rigorous truthfulness is the only thing that can lead to genuine self-knowledge. So we cultivate the art of self-examination "to surrender our destructive, maladaptive life patterns to God so that we can become more fully the person God intends."[15]

According to Thompson, four particular principles govern this "life review."[16]

1) Examination of conscience is a process that takes a long time. So be patient as well as honest with yourself.
2) Shining a bright light on areas of your life previously uninspected will be uncomfortable. So acknowledge your fear, guilt, shame, and embarrassment without letting them control you.
3) Some areas of darkness in your life will not become visible immediately and will remain resistant to your own efforts to expose them. So rely on God's grace to provide the insight you need at the right time.
4) Self-examination is just that—examination of you, and not a focused attention on what others have done to you. So keep the focus on yourself.

It is important to remember, as well, that you are not alone in this journey. Although difficult at times, this is a well-worn path. Wise spiritual pilgrims have preceded us and cheer us on.

"Conscience," claims Jim Forest, "is God's whispering voice within us calling us to a way of life that reveals God's presence and urges us to refuse actions that destroy community and communion."[17] Given the fact that it is often a struggle to hear the quiet voice of our conscience, spiritual guides throughout the history of the church have identified tools that help open our ears. The Ten Commandments provide one of the most helpful starting points. They provide a basic framework for you to examine your actions, words, and attitudes. The Beatitudes—known as the commandments of blessedness in the Orthodox tradition—establish a standard that will prick everyone's conscience. You can also examine your conscience by the measure of the fruit of the Spirit—love, joy, peace, patience, kindness, goodness, faithfulness, gentleness, and self-control—nine attributes of faithful discipleship identified by Paul in Galatians 5:22-23.

A number of prayers have been used throughout the history of the church, many of them very ancient, for the examination of conscience. Perhaps one of the most famous is that of Ephraim the Syrian, an early church father who exerted a profound influence on the lives of the Wesley brothers:

> O Lord and Master of my life, take from me the spirit of sloth, despair, lust for power and idle talk. But give to me, your servant, the spirit of chastity, humility, patience and love. O Lord and King, grant to me to see my own faults and not to condemn my brother and sister. For you are blessed unto the ages of ages.[18]

In his discussion of the examination of conscience, à Kempis admonishes: "Examine your conscience diligently, therefore, confessing the secrets of your heart so that God might cleanse you fully, leaving no barrier. . . . Offer your whole self upon the altar of your heart as a living sacrifice, holy and acceptable to God, to the honor of God's name."[19]

Contrition. The term *contrition* comes from a Latin word meaning "crushed to pieces." To be contrite means to be overcome with remorse, cut to the quick, devastated by a sense of personal responsibility for something hurtful, harmful, or destructive you have done. It means to be heartbroken. An authentic and sincere examination of conscience leads to a broken and contrite heart because it reveals to us just how far we have missed the mark. In Psalm 51, one of the most important lyrical expressions of penitence in the Old Testament, the psalmist's lament builds to this ultimate climax:

> O Lord, open my lips,
> and my mouth will declare your praise.
> For you have no delight in sacrifice;
> if I were to give a burnt offering, you would not be pleased.
> The sacrifice acceptable to God is a broken spirit;
> a broken and contrite heart, O God, you will not despise. (15-17, NRSV)

In a blog post on true contrition, George Simon observes:

> The contrite person has had their once haughty and prideful ego completely crushed under the tremendous weight of guilt and shame. Such a person has "hit bottom" (as 12-step program adherents are wont to say) not only because they can no longer bear the

> thought of how badly their actions hurt others but also because of their deep realization of how their usual way of doing things has resulted in abject personal failure.[20]

The Council of Trent classically defined contrition as "a sorrow of the soul and a detestation of the sins committed, with the firm determination not to sin again" (Sess. 14.4). Perhaps the most important aspect of this definition is its interior focus. More than words, or formulas, or actions, contrition resides in the heart.

Peter Storey has been a dear friend of many years. A native South African and leader within The Methodist Church there, he found himself in the epicenter of the struggle against apartheid. After the demise of this diabolical regime he served on the Truth and Reconciliation Commission, tasked to bring together victims and perpetrators of unspeakable atrocities in the quest for restorative justice. Daily he witnessed the drama of contrition and forgiveness. In a fascinating article on "Remorse, Forgiveness, and Rehumanization," Pumla Gobodo-Madikizela explores these stories of reconciliation.[21] She examines, in particular, the confession of Eugene de Kock, the apartheid government's chief assassin, and the empathy and forgiveness it elicits among his victims. She describes this dynamic interchange as the "paradox of remorse." Her research led her to the conclusion that genuine remorse humanizes perpetrators and transforms their evil from the unforgivable into something that can be forgiven. This is the power of contrition within the process of confession. Genuine remorse sets the stage, then, for the act of confession itself.

Confession. "No matter how often it happens," claims Jim Forest, "confession is one of life's most intimate events, far more revealing of who we are than taking off all our clothing. It is revealing out loud, to Christ . . . the ways we have lost the path that leads into the kingdom of God."[22] In his study of confession, he has collected stories about this sacrament in his Catholic tradition, and one in particular reveals a primary quality related to this action. One of his friends reminisced about a particular experience he had:

> I was worried that I might forget what I needed to confess so I made a list of my sins and brought it with me. The priest saw the paper in my hand, took it, looked through the list, tore it up, and gave it back to me. Then he said "Kneel down," and he absolved me. That was my confession even though I never said a word! But I felt truly my sins had been torn up and that I was free of them.[23]

The practice of confession liberates.

Within the Protestant tradition, most followers of Christ believe we have immediate access to God. All we need to do is confess our sins directly to God through the power of the Holy Spirit and God will forgive us, without any means or intermediaries. Some Catholic and Orthodox Christians argue that only a priest who has been vested with the "power of the keys" can forgive sins (see Matthew 16:19). We must confess, therefore, to an intermediary who provides a means of forgiveness that we can trust implicitly. Pope Francis, in *The Name of God Is Mercy*, offers this insight into the importance of this form of individual confession: "It is true that I can talk to the Lord and ask him for forgiveness, implore him. And the Lord will forgive me immediately. But it is important," he continues, "that I . . . sit in front of a priest. . . . There is objectivity in this gesture of genuflection before the priest; it becomes the vehicle through which grace reaches and heals me."[24] John Wesley understood this. He argued for both mediated and immediate encounters with God. God works both immediately in our lives—without any means whatsoever—but also through means that Christ has ordained, namely, those places where God has promised to meet us and heal us. God's primary desire is to heal and make new; God uses whatever means possible to help us experience grace and mercy in our lives.

In his exploration of the healing power of confession, Scott Hahn reflects on the idea of confession as covenant, something closely tied to Catholic practice. He brings all the themes of deliverance in Scripture to bear on this important practice.[25] The words of Paul in Romans (7:24-25, NRSV) function as his takeoff point for this larger conversation: "Who will rescue me from this body of death? Thanks be to God through Jesus Christ our Lord!" In the Hebrew Scriptures, God's relationship with the chosen people was deeply familial in nature; all the images of covenant revolved around this larger concept of an extended and united family. The biblical narrative reveals how God extends this family-covenant, renews covenant relationships, and restores this bond of love when it has been broken. Hahn concludes his discussion with this important insight about confession as covenant:

> Forgiveness is a great gift, but it's a penultimate gift. It's intended to prepare us for something still greater. Christians are saved not only *from* sin, but *for* sonship—divine sonship in Christ. We are not just criminals who have been exonerated; we are sons and daughters who have been adopted. We are children of God. . . . The essential effect of confession, then, is

> enabling our forgiveness so that we can be restored to Trinitarian life.[26]

Given this covenantal aspect of the practice of confession—its relationship-repairing character—the act of confession includes our effort to make amends or repair broken relationships.

Satisfaction. The idea of "making satisfaction" often scares Protestants. It connotes for them something that must be done in order to earn forgiveness. But this is far from the case. Rather, it is an element in this larger process of confession integral to contrition and the act of confession. It is part and parcel of reconciliation. We do well to remember that in almost all Twelve-Step programs of recovery, two steps involve the need to make things right with those you have hurt or wounded as a consequence of your brokenness. Step 8 involves making a list of all persons you have harmed and then determining to make things right. To fulfill Step 9, the person seeking recovery must make amends to such people wherever possible, except when to do so would injure them or others. As Father Compiani has observed, "God's forgiveness is not confined to the repentant sinner, but through him it radiates throughout the community by transforming interpersonal relationships."[27] Those who have confessed and have received the forgiveness of God become potential agents of reconciliation in the world, and this begins, first and foremost, with those they have wounded.

The story of Zacchaeus reveals the natural movement from confession/forgiveness to satisfaction. It exemplifies the way in which a change of heart begs for concrete acts of reparation in the real relationships of our lives. When Zacchaeus repented and received the gift of forgiveness from Jesus, he immediately stood up and declared: "Look, half of my possessions, Lord, I will give to the poor; and if I have defrauded anyone of anything, I will pay back four times as much. Then Jesus said to him, 'Today salvation has come to this house, because he too is a son of Abraham" (Luke 19:8-9, NRSV). Zacchaeus had abused his power and cheated people in his own community in order to benefit himself. But when he repented and found forgiveness, nothing could stop him from making amends with those he had abused. And Jesus could do nothing other than rejoice because Zacchaeus had found salvation and this simply burst out of him in an act of love rooted in the faith of Abraham.

Satisfaction has many forms. With regard to our judicial system we often say that the punishment should fit the crime. Likewise, in satisfaction, the act should fit the wound inflicted, the sin committed, or the wrong that has been done. On the most basic level it consists of a heartfelt apology and sincere desire to repair a relationship broken by your own words and actions. It may be as simple as reaching out to the one you have grieved in a simple effort to makes amends, as in the Twelve-Step programs. But wisdom about this aspect of the process of individual confession reveals that restitution—restoration for something lost or stolen, or recompense for an injury or loss—facilitates the process of healing and reconciliation for all involved. Forgiveness is something you receive from God or from someone else. This is a gift that heals your own soul. Restitution, restoration, reconciliation—these are more difficult because they extend beyond yourself and into the broken space between you and someone else. The effort to experience reconciliation is neither easy nor certain. All action in the direction of wholeness entails risk and, therefore, necessitates much prayer.

Absolution. Most Protestants tend to think about forgiveness or absolution in the same way they view the act of confession. Since we have immediate access to God's forgiveness through the redemptive work of Christ and the power of the Holy Spirit, we need no other mediator. God forgives the repentant sinner directly. God's grace is free and received freely as the Spirit bears witness with our spirits that we are the forgiven children of God. No one would argue against this. But in his discussion of confession, Richard Foster identifies a concern that has plagued many with regard to the human dimensions of this process of forgiveness.

> The person who has known forgiveness and release from persistent, nagging habits of sin through private confession should rejoice greatly in this evidence of God's mercy. But there are others for whom this has not happened. Let me describe what it is like. We have prayed, even begged, for forgiveness, and though we hope we have been forgiven, we sense no release. We doubt our forgiveness and despair at our confession.[28]

For those who relate to this conundrum, he offers these encouraging words from the *Book of Common Prayer*: "If there be any of you who by this means cannot quiet his own conscience herein but require further comfort or counsel, let him come to me or to some other minister of God's word, and open his grief."[29] Sometimes it is important to hear words of forgiveness, not simply in our hearts, but through the voice of a brother or sister who has heard our confession. Foster identifies three advantages to this formalized confession with absolution.[30] First, the tangible, relational quality of this experience precludes any excuses on our part. Second, the word of absolution is expected and spoken over the penitent sinner, and spoken words have power. Third, it moves us to a deeper appreciation of what he calls "the sinfulness of sin"—the seriousness of our sinful state as we reveal it to another human being. In his own "Diary of a Confession," Foster bears witness to the liberation that this experience of absolution brings.

In the papal document of Pope Francis that launched his famous Jubilee of Mercy in 2015, he discussed the importance of this human bond and vehicle of divine grace, and the critical role that those who hear the confessions of others play:

> Let us place the Sacrament of Reconciliation at the centre once more in such a way that it will enable people to touch the grandeur of God's mercy with their own hands. For every penitent, it will be a source of true interior peace.
>
> Let us never forget that to be confessors means to participate in the very mission of Jesus to be a concrete sign of the constancy of divine love that pardons and saves. . . . Confessors are called to embrace the repentant son who comes back home and to express the joy of having him back again. . . . In short, confessors are called to be a sign of the primacy of mercy always, everywhere, and in every situation, no matter what.[31]

Dietrich Bonhoeffer may have said it best:

> A man who confesses his sins in the presence of a brother knows that he is no longer alone with himself; he experiences the presence of God in the reality of the other person. As long as I am by myself in the confession of my sin everything remains in the dark, but in the presence of a brother the sin has to be brought into the light.[32]

Whether the Spirit speaks into the depths of your soul, "Your sins are forgiven"; or whether after hearing your confession a beloved friend prays a prayer of healing for all the sorrows and hurts of your past with the assurance of God's peace; or whether a priest proclaims these ancient words over you, "I absolve you from all censures and sins, in the name of the Father and of the Son and of the Holy Ghost"; all point to the same reality—God desires to forgive you fully through these human channels of grace.

Reflect on these words of the psalmist and let them speak peace to your soul:

> Bless the LORD, O my soul,
>   and all that is within me,
>   bless his holy name.
> Bless the LORD, O my soul,
>   and do not forget all his benefits—
> who forgives all your iniquity,
>   who heals all your diseases,
> who redeems your life from the Pit,
>   who crowns you with steadfast love and mercy. . . .
> The LORD is merciful and gracious,
>   slow to anger and abounding in steadfast love.
> He will not always accuse,
>   nor will he keep his anger forever.
> He does not deal with us according to our sins,
>   nor repay us according to our iniquities.

For as the heavens are high above the earth,
so great is his steadfast love toward those who fear him;
as far as the east is from the west,
so far he removes our transgressions from us.
As a father has compassion for his children,
so the LORD has compassion for those who fear him.
For he knows how we were made;
he remembers that we are dust. . . .

Bless the LORD, O you his angels,
you mighty ones who do his bidding,
obedient to his spoken word.
Bless the LORD, all his hosts,
his ministers that do his will.
Bless the LORD, all his works,
in all places of his dominion.
Bless the LORD, O my soul.
(Psalm 103:1-4, 8-14, 20-22, NRSV)

PRAYER RESOURCES FOR INDIVIDUAL CONFESSION

Here are some prayers of confession that might be helpful to you. They are drawn from the Roman Catholic and Methodist traditions, expressing the cry of the human heart.

O my God, I am heartily sorry for having offended Thee,
and I detest all my sins because of thy just punishments,
but most of all because they offend Thee, my God,
who art all good and deserving of all my love.
I firmly resolve with the help of Thy grace to sin no more
and avoid the near occasions of sin. Amen.[33]

Lord Jesus, Son of God,
have mercy on me, a sinner.[34]

God of wholeness and healing,
I bring you my brokenness and sinfulness, my fears
and my despair.
I lay it all at your feet.
Forgive me for all I have done to grieve you.
Forgive me for the ways in which I have alienated
myself from others and from you,
failing to embrace your will and your way.
Touch my heart, my head, and my hands that I might
rediscover the peace that only you can give.
In this holy moment flood me with your presence
and power.
God of wholeness and healing,
grant me faith and confidence that in this moment
my broken life can be made whole
as I open myself fully to your mercy and love.
Amen.[35]

Patient and Forgiving God,
I need to ask your forgiveness for much, although I
know I am your child.
You have forgiven me for everything in Christ, but
I continue to stumble and fall like a little child.
Christ reigns in my heart,
but pride emerges in the shadow of my spiritual
progress,
self-will, idolatry, and love of the world assault my
soul;
desire and love of praise, jealousy, and envy
crowd my thoughts.
I feel terrible about the darkness remaining in
my heart.
While my words and actions seem to be good and
pure,

my intentions and motives are sometimes
self-serving and
anything but godly. . . .
By your grace you free me from bondage to outward sin,
and the power of inward sin is broken while not entirely destroyed. . . .
But I need to experience your life-changing love over and over again in order to grow into the fullness of your love. Amen.[36]

PRACTICING INDIVIDUAL CONFESSION

Here are some exercises to help guide you with regard to your own practice of individual confession: the prayer of examen, a burning up your sins exercise, some guidance for pondering a hymn, and the assistance of a confessor.

Prayer of Examen. Ignatius of Loyola developed a practice known as the prayer of examen as part of his famous spiritual exercises. It combines our need to examine our conscience with the issue of our consciousness of God in life. It involves reflection, usually in the evening, with regard to the day past and usually includes five movements.[37]

1) Quiet yourself. The prayer of examen begins with a celebration of life and an expression of thanks to God.

2) Seek illumination. Pray for grace to see yourself clearly as you reflect and to see how God has been present in your day. Use a prayer like this one in this movement of the examen: "Lord, teach me where and how to find you in the midst of my life. I know that you are everywhere, and all day you are at work for good in the world; so open my eyes to see you every day."

3) Examine your life. Inventory the course of your day as if watching a video playback. Allow God to show you concrete instances of God's presence and guidance. Where do you perceive God at work?
4) Relinquish your brokenness. Review your spiritual health, and your need for cleansing, forgiveness, and healing. Pray the words of the psalmist (139:23-24, NRSV):

> Search me, O God, and know my heart;
> test me and know my thoughts.
> See if there is any wicked way in me,
> and lead me in the way everlasting.

5) Embrace God's grace. Give thanks to God for those events that evoke gratitude. Live in the resolve that tomorrow is another day, with fresh opportunities to love and serve. You may close your time of examen with a prayer like this one:

> You, eternal Trinity, are a deep sea: The more I enter you, the more I discover, and the more I discover, the more I seek you. . . . O abyss! O eternal Godhead! O deep sea! What more could you have given me than the gift of your very self? . . . Good above every good, joyous Good. Good beyond measure and understanding! Beauty above all beauty.[38]

Burning Up Your Sins. You can practice individual confession—simply confessing your own sins to God—anytime, anywhere, and without anyone else. This is between you and God, an expression of the most intimate relationship you will ever have in life. As we have seen, while it is sometimes helpful to have a human intermediary who can assist you in this act of confession, you also have an immediate connection to God through Christ in the power of the Spirit. God's grace can be mediated to you, in other words, through others, but means or methods are never absolutely necessary; you can connect directly with God at any time. But as we all know, actions speak louder than words. The practice of burning your sins puts words into action.

Sit quietly before God in a time of prayer. Enter into God's presence reverently and with the eager anticipation of God being ready and able to lift burdens off your shoulders and free you for more joyful living. Have a piece of paper and a pen or pencil available so you can write down those sins you want to confess. Also have some matches and a fireproof basin into which you can place burning paper. You may be entering into this experience with one very specific concern. Perhaps you wounded someone with your words or actions and are deeply grieved. You may be struggling with some aspect of brokenness in your life that has been troubling you for some time—an addiction, a pervasive attitude, a perennial failure. You are simply weary and have come to that point in time in which you must deal with it once and for all. On the other hand, there may be a whole range of concerns that occupies your mind over which you feel remorse. Whatever the circumstance, enter into this prayerful moment with the assurance that God knows you more deeply than you know yourself and seeks your healing.

Invite the Holy Spirit to help you articulate the sins you seek to confess. Don't rush into this, but deliberate over this in prayer. When you feel you are ready, write down that thing or those things that the Spirit brings to mind in a statement that simply begins, "Loving and forgiving God, I confess to you that I . . ." Or simply confess your sins in your own written words. Once you have completed writing out your confession, fold the paper, carefully light the paper with a match, and place it into the basin. As soon as the ashes have cooled, take the basin outside, if you are able, and blow the ash into the wind, praying this or some similar prayer from your heart:

> Thank you, O God, for the forgiveness you offer me in Jesus. Remove my guilt and shame, and through the power of your Spirit, give me a new start. Burn up all my sins in the immensity of your love and cast the ashes of my sins to the wind. Help me know in the depth of my being that in the name of Jesus Christ I am your forgiven and beloved child. Amen.

Pondering a Hymn. The Psalms in Scripture, hymns, and other sacred songs can be used for meditative use and prayer in addition to their normal use as sung texts in worship services. In the opening pages of this chapter I introduced you to some stanzas of a Charles Wesley hymn that are a helpful aid in individual confession. In this hymn he describes the human state as weary and burdened. Do you ever feel this way? Read through these two stanzas of the hymn again.

Weary of this war within,
  Weary of this endless strife,
Weary of ourselves and sin,
  Weary of a wretched life;

Burdened with a world of grief,
  Burdened with our sinful load,
Burdened with this unbelief,
  Burdened with the wrath of God

Take some time to ponder the questions that Wesley poses.

What wears you down?

- War within—What are the battles you are presently waging internally?
- Endless strife—Is there some continual struggle in which you are involved?
- Ourselves and sin—What have you said or done that has alienated you from God and others and continues to eat at you?
- A wretched life—What is it that makes you feel depleted and unfulfilled?

What weighs heavy upon you in life?

- A world of grief—What losses have you sustained that continue to burden you?
- Our sinful load—What sins do you carry around with you every day?
- Unbelief—What makes it difficult for you to entrust your life to Christ?
- Fear of God's wrath—What stands between you and God that fills you with fear?

While not all of these concerns relate directly to your sins or your sinfulness, all of them do create anxiety, leading to a sense of separation, alienation, and loneliness. These things create barriers between you and God and between you and others. These burdens hold you back from being your best self—the person God intends you to be as a beloved child. After you have pondered these questions, write down some of your thoughts, and then pray this prayer:

> Forgiving God, I come to you weary and burdened and seeking rest from all those forces that deplete my

life. Help me rest secure in the promise that you will give rest for my soul and free me for abundant life in Christ. Amen.

There are other hymns, of course, for you to ponder as well. Simply follow the same process with these hymns. Identify a concern that relates to you. Ponder it in your heart. Or simply read or sing the hymn stanza by stanza, pausing at the conclusion of each stanza to consider your sins, repent, and offer them to God, asking for forgiveness. Here are a few suggestions. Consider making this exercise a regular practice in your life of devotion.

Heal Me, Hands of Jesus (Michael Perry)
Heal Us, Emmanuel, Hear Our Prayer (William Cowper)
O Sacred Head Now Wounded (Anonymous)
When I Survey the Wondrous Cross (Isaac Watts)
Pass Me Not, O Gentle Savior (Fanny Crosby)
I Surrender All (J. W. Van Deventer)
Depth of Mercy (Charles Wesley)
Just as I Am, Without One Plea (Charlotte Elliott)
Alas! and Did My Savior Bleed (Isaac Watts)
O Crucified Redeemer (Timothy Rees)
Out of the Depths I Cry to You (Martin Luther)

Finding a Confessor. Protestants don't tend to use the term *confessor* for the person to whom they confess their sins, but this is a language commonplace to the Roman Catholic or Orthodox Christian. In those traditions, given their theology of the "power of the keys"—the authority of the priest to hear and absolve sins—every priest functions as a confessor. But this practice even there has fallen on hard times. One viable option to you, however, with regard to the ongoing confession of individual sins, involves finding a person to whom you can confess your sins in comfort and confidence. The famous Protestant apologist, C. S. Lewis, felt a strong aversion to "auricular confession"—the technical term for confession to a priest—because of the prejudices he harbored in early life against Roman Catholicism. He felt a strong attraction to this practice, however, and resolved to take it up. He actually described this as one of the most difficult decisions he had ever made. But once he broke through the mental impediments he had nurtured, he confessed regularly to an Anglican monk, and this became a life-sustaining practice for him.

In his study of confession, Jim Forest devotes an entire chapter to "Finding a Confessor."[39] He does not provide practical guidance as he reflects with others on the importance of people in our lives to whom we confess and become conduits of God's forgiveness. Without question, the primary concern in this regard relates to trust. Who can you trust? Who can you talk with and unburden your heart in confidence? Who do you know who has the spiritual capacity and depth to speak for Christ? Only you can answer these questions. But two possibilities present themselves immediately: your pastor and your dearest friends.

If you have interest in pursuing the idea of confessing your sins regularly to a confessor, first, broach this question with that friend or pastor after you have given it serious consideration. Spend some time talking with them about it. You might simply say, "I really feel I need someone with whom I can talk about my shortcomings, my failures, my sins with honesty and in confidence. I am at a point in my spiritual life in which I just know this would be so helpful. Would you consider being that person for me, or praying with me about it?" See then, under the guidance of the Holy Spirit, where this overture takes you.

Jim Forest concludes his chapter with this helpful and humorous story from one of his friends: "The dream priest [or spiritual friend] I'm looking for to hear my confession . . . is so saintly he walks barefoot on water without even noticing his feet are wet—and is deaf as a stone. Until I find him, I'll have to make do with one whose shoes are muddy and who understands only too well what I'm saying."[40]

Questions for Personal Reflection and Group Discussion

1. How do you define *sin*? How is sin understood, defined, and discussed in your worshiping community?

2. Spend time evaluating the three key relationships, as identified by Schmemann:
   a. Relationship to God
   b. Relationship to others
   c. Relationship to one's self

3. What actions of yours within each of these three relationships break your heart?

4. Through what means have you experienced God's forgiveness? Has it always been through silent/individual confession alone, or have you had others speak words of forgiveness aloud in response to your confession, either formally or informally?

5. Consider the difference between "making satisfaction" in order to gain forgiveness versus in response to being forgiven. How does your

65

exploration affect your understanding of this part of confession?

6. When have you offered restitution, recompense, or reconciliation for an offense? How was what you offered received?

7. Go back to page 58 and review the section "Practicing Individual Confession." If you have not already done so, identify one way to practice individual confession.

CHAPTER 3
Mutual Confession

> Confession is a discipline that functions within fellowship. In it we let trusted others know our deepest weaknesses and failures. This will nourish our faith in God's provision for our needs through his people, our sense of being loved, and our humility before our brothers and sisters. Thus we let some friends in Christ know who we really are, not holding back anything important, but, ideally, allowing complete transparency. We lay down the burden of hiding and pretending, which normally takes up such a dreadful amount of human energy. We engage and are engaged by others in the most profound depths of the soul.[1]

Thus the late Dallas Willard broached a conversation about confession in his discussion of some classical disciplines for spiritual life. He had become convinced over the years that the most critical growth Christians experience comes as the consequence of submission, primarily submission to one another in Christian *koinonia* (community or fellowship). If our own pride and sense of self-sufficiency are the primary impediments to spiritual health, it only makes sense that when we submit self to the scrutiny of someone else, as painful as that may be, genuine growth becomes a possibility. Authentic community entails mutual confession.

When Catherine Larson interviewed survivors of the Rwandan genocide and collected their stories for the preparation of her documentary, *As We Forgive*, the statement of one victim touched her deeply. "Forgiveness is a gift one gives," Joy declared, "to change the heart of the offender."[2] When we confess our sins to one another, it changes our hearts. We become the vehicles of God's transformative power. We participate with God in the drama of redemption and reconciliation. After discussing Joy's experience in greater depth, Larson concludes her narrative with these poignant words. Forgiveness offered to one another, she maintains,

> is a growing empathy for the shared humanity of the offender, a growing understanding that the decision itself will also release us, and a growing enlightenment as to the power and need of forgiveness in the world and in our hearts.
>
> Like any gift, forgiveness can bring joy to both the giver and the receiver, and the one who gives pays the highest price. But perhaps the extreme costliness of this particular gift imbues forgiveness, of all human actions, with the greatest potential to image forth the divine.[3]

Mutual confession immerses us in this grace-filled drama of redemption and joy.

SCRIPTURAL FOUNDATIONS OF MUTUAL CONFESSION

Two biblical texts stand out as foundations of mutual confession. They reflect what I will call the twin dimensions of this practice, the first having to do with discipline in the life of the church, the second with discipleship, particularly as it relates to growth in grace toward holiness.

Discipline: Confessing Sin Inside the Church. You and I fail each other in the community of faith. Through words and deeds we let each other down and need to repent our own brokenness. Our faith demands honesty and transparency in this regard. Sometimes malice festers inside local congregations, even leading to the destruction of the community. So to ignore this reality or to play down its danger can be catastrophic. All this begs the rather critical question: If we cannot forgive one another inside the community of faith, how can we ever hope to be a sign of reconciliation outside the confines of the church? In unique material within the Gospel of Matthew, therefore, Jesus instructs his followers about how to seek reconciliation within the community of faith given the nature of sin and its destructive power among its members:

> If another member of the church sins against you, go and point out the fault when the two of you are alone. If the member listens to you, you have regained that one. But if you are not listened to, take one or two others along with you, so that every word may be confirmed by the evidence of two or three witnesses. If the member refuses to listen to them, tell it to the church; and if the offender refuses to listen even to the church, let such a one be to you as a Gentile and a tax collector. (Matthew 18:15-17, NRSV)

Jesus' plan here reflects the wisdom of Deuteronomy (19:15) in terms of a peaceful way to resolve problems. And while the process outlined here may seem confrontational and the penalty for recalcitrance rather severe, restoration and reconciliation remains its ultimate goal.

The Gospel-writer sandwiches this text between teachings and parables about forgiveness. Coming immediately before are a warning about causing little ones to stumble and the parable of the ninety-nine sheep and the one who went astray. Both the teaching and the parable emphasize the importance of every person to God and the need to secure and restore them relationally. Immediately following his plan for forgiveness and restoration, Jesus reminds Peter about the parameters of forgiveness (namely, that it is beyond calculation) and, in his parable of the unforgiving servant, demonstrates our need to forgive others as God has forgiven us. All this instruction sets the Christian community apart from a world that embraces contrary values. As in the time of Jesus, many people today walk away from relationships easily rather than finding a way forward together. Concerned more about our own rights, we may too easily abandon our responsibility to each other.

Jesus outlines a clear, deliberate, and intentional process that binds people together in love and reconciliation. Patience and gentleness characterize the practice he envisions. "With a little more patience and little less temper," wrote Robert Lewis Stevenson, "a gentler and wiser method might be found in almost every case."[4] This sentiment certainly reflects the spirit of discipline within the community that Jesus intended. His plan of restoration could be viewed just as an aspect of individual confession if Jesus had not expanded the process progressively into the larger community. In essence, he demonstrates how my sin against anyone in the fellowship of faith almost always extends far beyond the level of that single relationship. As when a stone is thrown into a pond, a ripple effect occurs that may demand a larger conversation.

When I was teaching in Kenya I was privileged to have several conversations with the eminent African philosopher and theologian, John Mbiti, about processes related to sin and reconciliation in his context. In every instance, he described processes in which an incident involving just two people (the perpetrator and the victim) required the involvement of the entire community. "An injury to one," he once explained, "is an injury to all." That is why people would say "all of us have been wounded" if one member of their community was injured by someone's action. Sin within the community of faith injures the whole community and the whole community must be reconciled. Mbiti's African context reflects many of the cultural norms and concepts of the biblical world in which Jesus lived and from which we can learn. "The whole community," as Mbiti explained, "takes responsibility for the deed."[5]

Before turning our attention to the second form of mutual confession related to discipleship, I need to explore with you a peculiar form of discipline that was common in the early church but which has now disappeared almost entirely. Persons who committed particularly grievous sins in the fellowship of believers were often required to perform an act of public penitence known as *exomologesis* (a Greek word for "confession"). Tertullian of Carthage, an extremely significant early church father, wrote about this practice at the beginning of the third century in his monumental treatise *On Repentance*. Many in his day considered him to be the greatest authority on this subject. In his description of this ritual process the offender was rebuked publicly and then put on a rigorous course of penance and reformation that frequently included excommunication. According to Clebsch and Jaekle, confession became "a kind of medicine of humiliation, possessing power to make better men and better Christians, and as such demonstrating God's mercy."[6] John McNeill provides a terse explanation of this penitential discipline which "lays the sinner low only to raise him up again."[7] In his treatise, Tertullian warned the congregation against self-righteousness and the penitent about being overly ashamed because all believers belonged to God both in sin and in grace.

The public nature of *exomologesis* made it a particularly odious exercise for some, if not all, who were compelled to endure it. To many faithful Christians, the imposition of this practice before the entire community and the embarrassment it entailed seemed antithetical to the way of Jesus and the method of reconciliation outlined in Matthew's Gospel. Rather than being restorative, it felt overly punitive and easily fell prey to those who abused power. So this harsh form of mutual confession as discipline was short-lived. The church abandoned it as a practice inconsistent with the gospel vision of a community characterized by grace, mercy, and restoration. Regardless, the "hard work" of discipleship (something the church saw reflected in the practice of *exomologesis*, perhaps) has remained a perennial component of mutual confession throughout the history of the church.

Discipleship: Confessing Personal Sins to One Another. James 5:16 is the classic text around which this second dimension of mutual confession revolves: "Confess your sins to one another, and pray for one another, so that you may be healed. The prayer of the righteous is powerful and effective" (NRSV). This verse demonstrates how submitting oneself to Jesus Christ as his disciple entails two concrete actions and one clear consequence; mutual confession and mutual prayer lead to healing. Pope Francis reminds us that confessing to fellow Christians "is a way of putting my life into the hands and heart of someone else, someone who in that moment acts in the name of Jesus. It's a way to be real and authentic: we face the facts by looking at another person and not in the mirror."[8] Similarly, Dietrich Bonhoeffer writes:

> Christ became our Brother in order to help us. Through him our brothers and sisters have become Christ for us in the power and authority of the commission Christ has given to them. Our brothers and sisters stand before us as the sign of the truth and the grace of God. They have been given to us to help us. They hear the confession of our sins in Christ's stead and they forgive our sins in Christ's name. They keep the secret of our confessions as God keeps it. When I go to my brother or sister to confess, I am going to God.[9]

James 5:16 has probably stimulated more conversation about mutual confession than any other statement in Scripture. Biblical commentators throughout the centuries, from Origen to Elsa Tamez, reflect on the wisdom found in this admonition. John Calvin describes the way in which Jesus "connects mutual confession with mutual prayer" so that our intimacy with others advances our journey to God.[10] A significant early Methodist scholar, Adam Clarke, acknowledges the way in which this general instruction maintains the communion of saints. Moreover, the practice "tends much to humble the soul, and to make it watchful."[11] In his lecture on "Mutual Confession of Faults, and Mutual Prayer," Charles Finney identifies three primary benefits related to this practice: justice, peace, and self-respect.[12]

In her reflection on statements like this one attributed to Jesus, Gay Byron observes that "another way of understanding the call for wholeness is in a communal sense. According to James, one can understand the meaning of faith only in the context of a community of individuals striving to become 'mature' and 'complete.'"[13] Similarly, Elsa Tamez views this text as a keystone to the "scandalous message of James":

> Here the author offers advice to the oppressed and disoriented communities, some of whose members live with no consistency between their faith and their works. He advises the mutual confession of sins. This practice involves a process of self-criticism and personal and communal purification. It requires enough humility to bow our heads to let another pray for us. It means honesty and the confession of personal and collective sins, without fear, with the freedom of love.[14]

Mutual confession facilitates spiritual growth in these various dimensions.

Reflecting on this text and his own "holy experiment" in mutual confession, Dane Deatherage offers this wonderful testimony:

> When I sit down on those early Friday mornings to confess my sins with my friend Cale, my cup is full of coffee. My heart is full of shame. Sometimes I can barely eke out my secrets. But my confession does not pour into an empty room. Two blue eyes stare back into mine. A set of ears listen to my most dreadful secrets. I have been masquerading and moonlighting as a sinner when I am in fact a saint. And I am

> about to reveal my secrets to my brother in Christ. And naturally, I brace myself for judgment.
>
> Then all of the sudden, Cale reminds me, "Because of Christ's work on the cross, because of his resurrection, you are forgiven and free from sin." Through Christ's death and resurrection, God says, "You are forgiven!" Cale echoes the Word of God, and I am flabbergasted by the grace of Christ every time these words roll off his tongue.[15]

"Make this your common practice:" so Eugene Peterson translates James's statement in his *Message* Bible. "Confess your sins to each other and pray for each other so that you can live together whole and healed" (MSG). This may be the clearest and most helpful way to articulate the goal of the Christian life—to live together whole and healed—and mutual confession opens the door to this possibility. Throughout its history the church has understood the importance of mutual accountability and fellowship with others in this journey of faith.

HISTORIC PRACTICES OF MUTUAL CONFESSION

Within the life of the community of faith, mutual confession has found a home primarily in the context of the small group. From among the many examples in which this practice has been central, I want to explore with you its setting in Benedictine monasticism, the Wesleyan Revival, the East African Revival, and in Dietrich Bonhoeffer's vision of life together.

Benedictine Monasticism. I am an oblate of Mount Angel Abbey in Oregon. On its most basic level this means that I have agreed to follow the *Rule of St. Benedict* as best I can. My relationship with the community has been life-giving. I'll never forget talking with one of the monks about his decision to affiliate with that particular community, especially considering that this meant a lifelong commitment to stability there. He said that he had visited many different monasteries and felt really good about them all, but when he came to Mount Angel there were actually a number of the monks who "rubbed him the wrong way," as he put it. In his prayer about this, God made it clear to him that this was the place for him because living with them would "knock off his own edges" and teach him how to love more fully. The primary purpose of a Benedictine monastic community is to help men and women grow more fully into the image of Christ—to love as he loves, in humility with peace of heart.

St. Benedict's *Rule*, developed in the sixth century as a foundation for monastic communities across Europe, calls monks and nuns to a daily rhythm of attentiveness, obedience, and conversion of life. A statement from the penultimate chapter of the *Rule* epitomizes the nature of community in this tradition, offered up in the form of a prayer. "Let them offer the love of brother and sister selflessly to one another. Let them fear God lovingly, love their superior with sincere and humble love, prefer nothing whatsoever to Christ, and may he bring us together to everlasting life."[16] One simple phrase encapsulates the heart and core of Benedictine spirituality: *ora et labora* (prayer and work). Benedict structured daily prayer for the community in a rhythm that included eight different "Hours." Also known as the Opus Dei (work of God) or the Daily Office, this pattern of prayer includes a continuous reading of Scripture and saying or chanting the Psalms in community. The keynote of the

Benedictine way is balance, with no harsh extremes. "To read, to pray, to place oneself before God:" writes Columba Stewart, "the flow from one to the other is meant to be entirely natural."[17] Holiness consists in the proper balance of all these elements in life. "Listen" is the very first word of the *Rule* and the practice of attentiveness provides the perfect foundation for mutual confession. Those who follow St. Benedict's *Rule* listen in an effort to discern the new path Christ is always calling us to travel in a lifelong process that Benedict called *conversatiomorum* (conversion of life).

Benedict wrote specifically about confession of sins or faults in the *Rule*—many describe chapters 23-30 as a Benedictine "code of discipline" in this regard—but mutual confession actually pervades this manual for growth in love and holiness. Esther de Waal describes Benedict's penetrating insight in this regard.

> Benedict wants the monk to realize the communal dimension of his fault and so that what is at issue is a question of social responsibility as well as individual responsibility. He sees sin as deep, structural, and pervasive, tying the individual and the corporate together. It must not be buried and denied, but exposed, and lived with in terms of repentance and new life.[18]

The abbot, of course, played a major role in this ongoing life of confession, but the responsibility that the members of the community had for one another in this regard was quite remarkable. "A common confession of faults," explains Stewart, ". . . within a communal setting (the so-called 'chapter of faults') were the customary means for the avowal of public failures."[19]

Stewart observes that for Benedict "the key to monastic life was accountability to God and to other people. Accountability galvanizes community, marking the difference between mere cohabitation and genuinely common purpose."[20] Often using the images of sickness, disease, and healing with regard to sin, Benedict stresses the divine therapy that those within the community offer to one another. Chapter 44 offers a very graphic depiction of discipline for those the abbot has prohibited from participation in both the Daily Office and Holy Communion. Such treatment was reserved only for the most serious offences. Such an offender was "to prostrate himself in silence at the oratory entrance at the end of the celebration of the Work of God. He should lie face down at the feet of all as they leave the oratory, and let him do this until the abbot judges he has made satisfaction."[21] De Waal reflects on the power of this act:

> To lie prostrate is an act of humiliation, of course, but it is also a symbolic act of touching the ground, being in touch with the ground of my being, the ground of the universe. . . . True repentance and restoration can never be a superficial matter. I find it illuminating to read this chapter in the context of the four-step return of the excommunicated in the early Church: mourn, listen, prostrate, stand. All those elements are here, and if I think about them as steps in a process, I see that in the end it all comes back to the desire of Benedict that I may stand—stand upright before God, stand in my proper place, amongst the people to whom I belong.[22]

In the Benedictine curriculum for growth in Christ, the practice of mutual confession played a major role and provided a model of accountability for future generations.

The Wesleyan Revival. John and Charles Wesley birthed Methodism as a movement of renewal in the eighteenth-century Church of England. Their vision revolved primarily around the idea of accountable discipleship. They shared many of the same concerns reflected in Benedictine spirituality. In this small group movement, the Wesleys developed "band meetings" (on the model of small groups in the heritage of Continental Pietism and English Societies) for the purpose of mutual confession. In his *Plain Account of the People Called Methodists*, John Wesley described the benefits of small accountability groups:

> Great and many are the advantages which have ever since flowed from this closer union of the believers with each other. They prayed for one another, that they might be healed of the faults they had confessed—and it was so. The chains were broken, the bands were burst in sunder, and sin had no more dominion over them. Many were delivered from the temptations out of which till then they found no way to escape. They were built up in our most holy faith. They rejoiced in the Lord more abundantly. They were strengthened in love, and more effectually provoked to abound in every good work.[23]

He made it clear that the primary purpose of mutual confession—or any form of confession for that matter—is for us to become "more and more dead to sin" and "more and more alive to God."[24]

While Methodism had a number of different small group structures, mutual confession took place primarily in the band meetings, which were formally organized in December 1738. Again, reflecting a pattern very similar to that within monasticism, Wesley developed a set of rules for those who desired to speak "freely and plainly" about the true state of their souls. This involved telling their fellow band members about the faults they had committed "in thought, word, or deed" and the temptations they had felt since the last meeting. The purpose of the bands, according to Wesley, was "to obey that command of God, 'confess your faults one to another, and pray one for another that ye may be healed' [James 5:16]."[25] Even before being permitted to join a band, those who were interested in participating were asked a number of probing questions:

1. Have you the forgiveness of your sins?
2. Have you peace with God, through our Lord Jesus Christ?
3. Is the love of God shed abroad in your heart?
4. Do you desire to be told of your faults?
5. Do you desire that every one of us should tell you, from time to time, whatsoever is in his heart concerning you?
6. Do you desire that in doing this we should come as close as possible, that we should cut to the quick, and search your heart to the bottom?[26]

In these small groups of four to seven members, divided by gender and marital status into bands for married men, single men, married women, or single women, they addressed another specific set of questions on a weekly basis:

1. What known sins have you committed since our last meeting?
2. What temptations have you met with?

3. How [were] you delivered?
4. What have you thought, said, or done, of which you doubt whether it be sin or not?
5. Have you nothing you desire to keep secret?[27]

David Lowes Watson, one of the experts on these accountability structures, observed: "Clearly this was a process of mutual confession, and for those who took their discipleship seriously, as did the members of these early societies, it was a significant point of accountability."[28]

Many of the early Methodist people bore witness to the importance of this mutual confession in their faith journeys, which led to deeper experiences and expressions of love. They offer compelling personal evidence of the spiritual benefits experienced in these small groups. The testimony of John Oliver illustrates the experience of a band meeting in this regard:

> Our society was now much united together, and did indeed love as brethren. Some of them had just began to meet in band, and invited me to meet with them. Here, one of them speaking of the wickedness of his heart, I was greatly surprised; telling them, I felt no such things, my heart being kept in peace and love all the day long. But it was not a week before I felt the swelling of pride, and the storms of anger and self-will: so when I met again, I could speak the same language with them. We sympathized with each other, prayed for each other, and believed, God was both able and willing to purify our hearts from all sin.[29]

According to Kevin Watson the band was the small group experience "where the most candid, direct, and searching conversations occurred related to the particularities of how people were falling short of the holiness that they were called to enter into as Christians."[30] Mutual confession in these groups not only helped expose personal brokenness but also provided the support and encouragement people needed to grow more fully into the image of Christ.

The East African Revival. During my years of teaching at St. Paul's United Theological College in Limuru, Kenya, my family and I enjoyed the weekly meeting of "The Fellowship" that took place every Thursday evening. The lively singing and the time of testimony, in particular, captivated us. Not a lot of confession took place in the actual time of fellowship, but we understood that an opportunity for this preceded the event and involved a small group within the Fellowship community. The roots of this practice can be traced directly to the East African or Balokole ("the saved ones") Revival. This movement, arguably the most influential Christian revival in twentieth-century Africa emerged in the 1930s as an attempt to revitalize the Anglican Church of Uganda from what many indigenous members considered to be its spiritual formalism and dry, arid orthodoxy. The particular marks of the Revival were its emphases on human sinfulness, public confession, and fellowship, all within the larger vision of "walking in the light."

When the East African Revival emerged as a distinct movement, one of its most noticeable and controversial characteristics was the pervasive practice of public confession of personal sins. Jason Bruner, a widely recognized expert on the Revival, has probed the cultural, social, and theological elements of this practice.[31] Those who were converted in the context of the Revival viewed the change in their lives as something much larger than their individual acceptance of a new faith. Their culture and communal orientation helped them understand that conversion necessarily entailed a variety of social ramifications as well. The effect of this was that the Revival made public many of these sins the revivalists had kept hidden. "Confession was the solution to secrecy," claims Bruner, "because naming sins in public brought them into the light. Secrecy protected the hidden world of conflicted and colluded spiritualities, and Balokole wanted a purified community of the saved."[32]

Confessions ranged from the stealing of objects or money from mission stations to heinous acts of violence. Revivalists were taught to root out any hint of sin from their own lives and often took the next step of publicly identifying others' sins as well. But Bruner has demonstrated how public confession and "walking in the light" were lived experiences and practices that led to joyful, innovative forms of personal and communal identity.[33] This may very well have been the case because the practice of public confession in the context of a "family" group set in motion the need to put things right. Restoring broken relationships and making restitution became the focus of their life and vision rather than the sins that had disrupted the life of the community. Like the early Methodists, they believed that the consequences of conversion ought to be evident in their changed attitudes and behavior. Bruner concludes that "public confession had a deep hold among African Balokole. It was a powerful, transformative, and salvific experience to reveal one's sins before others."[34]

This revival movement demonstrates the power of mutual confession in the context of a community. Balokole public confession affected the revivalists in two particular ways: 1) this practice enabled the Holy Spirit to break the power of sin in their lives so they could walk in the light, and 2) it drew them into a safari of reconciliation, simultaneously restoring old communities and establishing new ones.

Bonhoeffer's Vision. Joshua Kaiser argues that "it is only through the practice of mutual confession that one enters into a place of communion with Christ at the altar."[35] Undoubtedly, this inextricable connection between penitence and sacrament led Dietrich Bonhoeffer to conclude his study of *Life Together* with a conversation about "Confession and Communion." The sacrament of Communion, more than any other action in the Christian community, "grounds" us in real life. Our meeting with Christ at the altar propels us into the world in witness and in service. If confession "makes us honest" about ourselves, Communion similarly makes us honest about our hunger and our need to offer bread to others. Those who live in Christ, according to Bonhoeffer, do not escape from the difficulties of this world by rising above it into some ethereal plain. Rather, faith anchors us firmly in a life that is "in but not of this world."

Based upon an exacting study of Bonhoeffer's vision of the Christian life in community in this regard, Kaiser identifies two potential trajectories that a spiritual practice like mutual confession can take. On one hand, such an exercise can act as an escape from reality by leading us into an "unreal world" of "spiritual ecstasy" (an interior life detached from the real world). Alternatively and properly, it can lead us more deeply into the "real world of God" out of which we "enter into the day's activities."[36] A deep and real connection with God, enhanced by mutual confession, must be incarnated necessarily in the real world in which we live. To put this very simply, your personal, inner life must find expression in your public, outer life. Christians fall perennially into the trap of being so heavenly minded that you are no earthly good, and Bonhoeffer understood this fully. Mutual confession helps us avoid this conundrum. This practice "is not a human achievement," according to Kaiser, "but a humble participation in Christ, who conforms Christians ever more into the divine image."[37] It entails a bold trust in Christ and a joyful daring.

PRACTICE OF MUTUAL CONFESSION

Mutual confession infers community. So all the suggestions related to this practice for this chapter involve small groups of one form or another.

Prayer for the Community of Faith. John Wesley's exposition of Matthew 18:15-17 is included among his so-called "Standard Sermons." The prayer below is a translation of the essence of the sermon into the form of a prayer. In the context of a small group, pray this prayer together.

Divide up the reading of the prayer so that each member of the small group has an opportunity to read a section. Simply following around in the circle works well. After the reader has read his or her respective section, a lengthy pause should follow to provide space for reflection. Following this period of silence, and after the reader says, "Forgive us, we pray," the group responds by saying, "Plant a spirit of reconciliation within us." Continue through the prayer until you have prayed it in its entirety.

God of Reconciliation,

You have called us to be ambassadors of healing and understanding in Christ. Yet it is easy for us to make ourselves feel good by pointing out failures in others. We talk about others behind their back. We are so frequently unfair.

Forgive us, we pray.
Plant a spirit of reconciliation within us.

When others within our community of faith have made mistakes or turned their back on you, rather than approaching them with a spirit of tender love, gentleness, and meekness, we nurture pride and contempt in our heart. Rather than dealing with our brothers and sisters directly and with genuine concern, we gossip and judge.

Forgive us, we pray.
Plant a spirit of reconciliation within us.

Lord, we need to help one another in our journey of faith, and all of us make many mistakes and get lost along the way. All of us need to learn gentleness, patience, and kindness from one another. Love ought to determine how we deal with our brothers and sisters in your family. Everyone needs to be understood, and often we need the counsel of others who see what we are doing better than we see for ourselves. We need to be accountable to one another because that is the only way we can continue to grow in your love.

Forgive us, we pray.
Plant a spirit of reconciliation within us.

We are a part of your community, the church. The whole point of our common life together is learning how to love and then sharing that love with everyone you bring into our path. Whenever we hurt one another by our words or our actions, move us toward reconciliation quickly. Help us to be honest with one another but always to speak the truth in love. We want to be your faithful family of healing and of love.

Forgive us, we pray.
Plant a spirit of reconciliation within us. Heal our broken relationships and make us one in Christ our Lord. Amen.[38]

Having prayed this prayer together, ask the following questions and engage in conversation as a small group about them:

- Which segment of the prayer touched me most deeply? And why?
- How might we be more faithful to God's vision of the community of faith?

Close with the ancient prayer of Richard of Chichester:

O most merciful redeemer, friend, and brother,
may we know you more clearly,
love you more dearly,
and follow you more nearly,
day by day. Amen.[39]

"Gather the Week" Exercise. One way to engage in mutual confession is to share an experience of "gathering the week." The idea for this practice comes from the work of Ben Campbell Johnson.[40] The exercise provides an opportunity for you to incorporate the confession of sins into an expanded life of prayer that relates directly to the ordinary events and decisions of your daily life. It includes both time for individual

reflection and then for sharing with others in the context of a small group and consists of five movements. You conduct the first three movements as individuals in the comfort of your own home in a way that is meaningful and helpful to you. You engage the final two movements together as a small group in a weekly meeting set at a convenient time for all involved. For the purposes of this exercise, the group should be no more than four people and may be as small as two. Set aside an hour or hour and a half on the same day each week to meet for reflection and prayer.

THREE INDIVIDUALIZED MOVEMENTS

Set aside time each day in the evening prior to retiring for the night to review the events of the day and your response to them. Alternatively, you can make a review of the previous day the following morning if you prefer.

1. Gather the day. Identify two or three significant events of your day (good or bad). Simply list those things that come immediately to mind, that are right on the surface of your consciousness or "on your heart."

2. Review the day. Reflect upon each of the events you have listed, reviewing your response to them. Think about words you spoke or actions you took. Are there any events concerning which you feel grieved, either in terms of your own words or actions, or those spoken about you or to you? Are there any ways that you have wounded others? In any of these events do you feel sorrow for what you said or did, or what you left unsaid or undone? As you conclude this aspect of the exercise, ask God to forgive you for anything in which you have failed to be God's faithful child.

3. Give thanks for the day. Take time to thank God for each part of your day, for your life, and for God's presence in the midst of it all. Consider those events you have listed and ask yourself where you see God as a healing or reconciling presence in them. Write down a brief prayer of thanks to God.

TWO SMALL GROUP MOVEMENTS
4. Confess your sins. From among the many experiences you have written about and reflected upon during your individual time from the previous week (since you last met), write down two or three actions or events from which you need to be unburdened. You might be able to capture each in a single word or phrase. Despite the fact that you have already confessed these matters before God and sought forgiveness and even feel relief, to share these with your friends can be extremely helpful. Simply and honestly share these concerns one by one around the circle. Pray for one another about each concern, and speak words of assurance and peace to one another, such as: "In the name of Jesus Christ, you are forgiven."
5. Seek the meaning. After you have had an opportunity to confess, pray, and receive the liberating words of forgiveness in Christ from one another, reflect together on the larger significance of these events in your life. Each person identifies, writes down, and talks about just one event or issue in this regard. Ask yourselves the following questions in turn: What is God saying to me in this event? What am I being called to do? How is this connected to the rest of my life? After you have each had an opportunity to share, pray for one another that God through the power of the Holy Spirit will confirm the insight and enable you to grow more fully into the image of Christ.

Life Together Exercise. The following exercise is based on Dietrich Bonhoeffer's classic book, *Life*

Together, referenced throughout this volume, and a study guide of this text written by David Ziemer of the Ekklesia Project.[41] This diverse group is a network of Christians who rejoice in a peculiar kind of friendship rooted in our common love of God and the church. This exercise includes reflection on pertinent biblical texts and exploration of how mutual confession can be experienced in local congregations.

Christ invites us to move beyond the boundaries of our individual lives into the shared reality of Christian community. The vision of Christ was for this new family into which we are baptized to practice radical togetherness. In a small group explore the following biblical texts that use the language of "one another" (*allelon* in Greek). The church is meant to be a community of persons who welcome one another (Romans 15:7), are servants of one another (Galatians 5:13), bear with one another lovingly (1 Thessalonians 5:11), love one another from the heart (1 Peter 1:22), confess our sins to one another (James 5:16), and forgive one another (1 Corinthians 2:13).

Address the following questions in your small group:

- Which of these have you experienced in your congregation?
- Which would you like to see more of?
- Which are harder to practice than others? Which are easier?
- What in your local congregation promotes and enables the practice of radical togetherness described in these passages? What blocks it?

Perhaps none of the passages for reflection here is more challenging—and more needed—than this:

"Confess your sins to one another . . . that you may be healed" (James 5:16, NRSV). None points better to the radical nature and need of Christian community in our time. Reflect on the following questions in the light of your study of this text in particular.

- What is the practice of confession and forgiveness like in the life of your congregation? Where and when does it occur? Who is involved?
- There is evidence that in the seminary community for which Bonhoeffer wrote *Life Together* many of his students initially felt very uncomfortable with the introduction of person-to-person confession and forgiveness.
- How comfortable is your congregation with the notion of confessing personal sins or faults to a fellow member?
- Can you share an example of when confession happened in your church? What difference did it make?
- Confessing sin to another person in a community seems to assume a deep level of closeness. Only with such intimacy can people welcome, understand, and forgive others in the name of Jesus.
- Where and in what contexts do such relationships exist in your congregation?
- What would need to change for this practice to grow?

A Wesleyan Small Group Experience.[42] Covenant Discipleship Groups developed as part of an effort to reclaim some of the characteristics and values of the original Wesleyan Revival and its small group structures. In particular, they were an adaptation of the early Methodist class meeting. These groups were slightly larger than the bands discussed earlier in this chapter. Generally, they consisted of about twelve members including both women and men, and even sometimes children. They were less intense, perhaps, than their smaller counterpart in the band—more oriented to fellowship than deep introspection, but oriented nonetheless on making disciples of Jesus. So the primary purpose of the Covenant Discipleship Group today is to help the congregation live into its mission of forming members into faithful disciples of Jesus Christ who live as his witnesses in the world.

Covenant Discipleship Groups are open to anyone in a community of faith who is ready to be accountable for their daily walk with Jesus Christ in the world. They are for persons who are willing to devote one hour every week to life in a small group, the purpose of which is to give an account of what they have done, or not done, to witness to Jesus Christ in the world and follow his teachings through acts of compassion, justice, worship, and devotion under the guidance of the Holy Spirit. Members of Covenant Discipleship Groups understand that their mission is to build up the body of Christ by watching over one another in love.

I suggest that you seriously consider introducing Covenant Discipleship Groups to your congregation, but I acknowledge that this kind of undertaking requires much preparation, prayer, and perseverance. The natural impulse will be to treat Covenant Discipleship Groups like a program and simply offer the groups as one group among a menu of others. If you want your congregation to form the needed leaders in discipleship, this impulse must be resisted. You will need to gain the support and help of your pastor(s) and other key leaders. Two resources are of particular help in this journey. Start with David Lowes Watson's book, *Covenant Discipleship: Christian Formation through Mutual Accountability*. The first half of the book provides a brief review of the theological, biblical, and historical foundations of these accountability groups. The second half of the volume is a practical guide for organizing Covenant Discipleship Groups, writing a covenant of discipleship or rule of life, leading a weekly meeting, and answering common questions and objections. Ideally, everyone in the group should have a copy of this book.

A second important resource is *Forming Christian Disciples: The Role of Covenant Discipleship and Class Leaders in the Congregation*, also by Watson. This volume is really designed for pastors and congregational leaders. The primary purpose of this book is to demonstrate how Covenant Discipleship fits into a "disciple-making system." This book also includes practical advice and suggestions for supporting and sustaining this ministry over time.

Kevin M. Watson (not related to David) has also done exceptional work with regard to reintroducing band and class meetings into congregational life. See his two helpful guides: *The Class Meeting: Reclaiming a Forgotten (and Essential) Small Group Experience* (2013) and *The Band Meeting: Rediscovering Relational Discipleship in Transformational Community* (2017). He also offers *A Blueprint for Discipleship* (2009) based upon John Wesley's General Rules as a guide for Christian living that can help place these small groups into the larger context of faithful discipleship.

While Covenant Discipleship Groups represent something of a "larger project" related to mutual confession, it will bear great fruit.

Questions for Personal Reflection and Group Discussion

1. Have you ever engaged in a practice of mutual confession? What did you take away from your experience?

2. Does your church value, teach, and model the practice of mutual confession? If not, why do think mutual confession is not a part of your community?

3. What is your understanding of the historical traditions explored in this chapter: Benedictine Monasticism, Wesleyan Revival, East African Revival, and Bonhoeffer's *Life Together*? Have you read or studied any of these traditions? Are there traditions you'd like to learn more about?

4. Do you have a person or group with which you could practice mutual confession? If you are studying this text in a small group, this might be a good place to start, or it might not. Consider the practical advice given in the section "Practice of Mutual Confession" (beginning on page 85) as you discern the people with whom you can confess.

5. Were you ever a part of a Covenant Discipleship Group? Are you still? What stories and relationships stand out to you from your experience?

CHAPTER 4

Communal Confession

Alongside the practices of individual and mutual confession, the worshiping community practices communal confession as it relates to the church as a whole. Those who worship in our churches today, I fear, may miss the significance of this corporate act. As individuals we need to confess our sins; we understand this. But the community of God's people—the church—also sins and needs to hear God's word of forgiveness and to experience spiritual liberation. In worship we acknowledge who God is and who we are in relationship to this God of love and grace. All our needs and all God's promises meet in this sacred liturgical space. In the movement to communal confession, our prayer shifts, as it were, from "forgive my sins" to "forgive our sin."

David deSilva observes that the plural pronoun in this statement "capture[s] our 'solidarity in corporate sinfulness,' including the sin that is woven into the society of which we are a part."[1] In the context of the liturgy—a word that literally means the "work of the people"—the mystery of who God is interfaces with the mystery of who we are; we, God's children, meet our God, experiencing the reality of forgiveness and liberation in a family bound together and set apart. As the community comes face-to-face with God in worship, that intimate communion cannot help but remind us of our sinful nature in addition to our various sins. "The corporate practice of confession," according to Ted Jennings, "teaches us to see. It teaches us to see ourselves in the light of God's action and promise. The practice of confession is practice in the banishment of illusion, of self-deception, of dishonesty. It is practice in honesty, in telling the truth."[2]

In communal confession, then, we acknowledge our failure to be God's people, recognize our sin as a community of faith, and repent (turn back) to God so that God can re-member and restore us as a living community of love in the world. This acknowledgment of the church's need (and not just that of individuals) to repent, confess, and receive God's forgiveness has deep roots in the scriptural witness.

SCRIPTURAL FOUNDATIONS FOR COMMUNAL CONFESSION

Old Testament scholars have categorized seven psalms as penitential psalms or psalms of confession (6, 32, 38, 51, 102, 130, 143). These songs not only provide a model for individual confession (we examined Psalm 51, for example, under that rubric), they also provide a template for communal confession. The primary context of the performance of these psalms is the whole people of God at worship. Psalm 130 may be the most well-known of these songs. In response to the tremendous majesty of God experienced among the Hebrews in worship, those who worship express the deepest yearning of the community for healing and liberation:

> Out of the depths I cry to you, O LORD.
>   Lord hear my voice!
> Let your ears be attentive
>   to the voice of my supplications!

If you, O Lord, should mark iniquities,
Lord, who could stand?
But there is forgiveness with you,
so that you may be revered.

I wait for the Lord, my soul waits,
and in his word I hope;
my soul waits for the Lord
more than those who watch for the morning,
more than those who watch for the morning.

O Israel, hope in the Lord!
For with the Lord there is steadfast love,
and with him is great power to redeem.
It is he who will redeem Israel
from all its iniquities. (NRSV)

The psalm transitions from the first person singular, "Out of the depths I cry," to the concluding acclamation, the Lord "will redeem Israel from all its iniquities." Caught up in the realities of sin, the community of faith itself yearns for forgiveness because of the many ways in which it too has "grieved the Holy Spirit."

Despite the fact that this phrase about sin grieving the Spirit occurs only twice in Scripture (Isaiah 63:10 and Ephesians 4:30), it expresses so potently the deep wound inflicted by human rebellion and the depth of alienation between God and God's children. Father Compiani provides a trenchant analysis of this language in his discussion of the "sacrament of mercy."[3] In Isaiah 63 the prophet condemns the rebellion of the Israelites against their God, but particularly their attitude of autonomy and self-sufficiency despite God's gracious provision for them. Their primary sin is the denial of their authentic role as the chosen of God and their exchange of election for service for election to privilege. Similarly, the writer to the church at Ephesus finds it reprehensible that the Christians there would act in ways that deny their baptismal (covenantal) identity.

Having been incorporated into God's saving plan and gifted with the Holy Spirit, their behavior toward one another betrays their practical allegiance to other gods.

> And do not grieve the Holy Spirit of God, with which you were marked with a seal for the day of redemption. Put away from you all bitterness and wrath and anger and wrangling and slander, together with all malice, and be kind to one another, tenderhearted, forgiving one another, as God in Christ has forgiven you. (Ephesians 4:30-32, NRSV)

They have abandoned their vocation as ambassadors of reconciliation—their calling to live as an alternative community of love and justice in the world. Called to be a model of reconciliation, in fact, they have forgotten how to forgive. Like the ancient Israelites, they disavowed their true identity. They compromised their witness that should have radiated "throughout the community by transforming interpersonal relationships . . . imparting to the whole Church a lifestyle that characterizes her as 'people of God.'"[4]

John's warning, directed to the same church in Ephesus, describes their dire circumstance in more graphic terms:

> But I have this against you, that you have abandoned the love you had at first. Remember then from what you have fallen; repent, and do the works you did at first. If not, I will come to you and remove your lampstand from its place, unless you repent.
>
> (Revelation 2:4-5, NRSV)

God calls the church to repentance, to confess its failure to be the community of light God intended it to be. Over against the signs of this fallenness—the five symptoms of sinful malice in Ephesians 4:31 (NRSV): bitterness, wrath, anger, wrangling, and slander—Paul calls the community of faith back to its true vocation. To live in the Spirit for the sake of the world, he argues, means to manifest the signs of redemption: "By contrast, the fruit of the Spirit is love, joy, peace, patience, kindness, generosity, faithfulness, gentleness, and self-control. There is no law against such things" (Galatians 5:22-23, NRSV). When the church is faithful in these things, it both announces and enacts God's grace and love to the world. Failure to do so mandates communal confession. Given the nature of the church's failure in this regard, its need sometimes seems even greater than that of the world outside.

Edwina Gateley, founder of the Volunteer Missionary Society in 1969, moved from the security of a hermitage to the pain and injustice of the streets of Chicago, sharing the good news of God's love in the brothels of the city. Her journal and poetry often indict the church and call for the repentance of the community of faith. On January 6, 1983, she wrote:

> I am beginning to believe that it is not the prostitutes who need the Church, but the Church which needs the prostitutes.
>
> God sends me to the prostitutes
> Because we, the Church,
> Are so hungry,
> So bewildered,
> So proud.
> We are in need,
> And only the "sinners,"
> The prostitutes,

And those who have no cause
To be proud
And self righteous
Can help us find
Our way again.[5]

Communal confession has to do with our acknowledgment of the many ways in which we have failed to be the church and have been complicit with evil. Until we repent and receive healing through the Spirit, we will never be the community of faith and light God has called us to be. Fortunately, the church has always been blessed with those who recognize the need for lament and have given expression to the possibility of restoration and renewal through the worship of God's people.

HISTORIC EXPRESSIONS OF CONFESSION IN CORPORATE WORSHIP

One of the five benefits of liturgical prayer that Richard Foster identifies in *Prayer: Finding the Heart's True Home* relates to the way in which it resists the privatization of religion, reminding us of our place within the larger context of the whole people of God.[6] In corporate worship we confess, repent, hear, and speak absolution. This is what Ted Jennings describes as "an abiding form of our life together and in the world. It is not something we finish in order to go on to something else. It is the constantly renewed beginning of all of our life."[7] Within the context of the historic worship of the church many different forms of communal confession have arisen that give expression to this concern.

The Service of Word and Table. The liturgy for the sacrament of Communion of The United Methodist

Church beautifully illustrates the centrality of communal confession and how its performance re-forms us into the people of God.[8] The sequence of Invitation, Confession, Words of Assurance, and Peace are incorporated into this normative and formative pattern for Eucharistic worship. It is interesting to note that this formal structure for communal confession generally follows a recitation of the Apostles' Creed, one of those confessions of faith we reflected upon in Chapter 1. So the structure of the liturgy in and of itself affirms the intimate connection between our affirmations about God and our confession of sin.

First, the church engages in communal confession as a response to an invitation. As in all things, God remains preeminent. God takes the first step toward us. If our hearts and lives are open to God—receptive to the grace God offers—then we respond in hope and expectation. The leader invites the community with these words:

> Christ our Lord invites to his table all who love him,
> who earnestly repent of their sin
> and seek to live in peace with one another.
> Therefore, let us confess our sin before God and one another.[9]

Several aspects of this introduction to the process of confession and pardon are noteworthy. First, Christ issues the invitation and love motivates our meeting him and one another at the table. The context of repentance and forgiveness is a meal, one of the most intimate activities we share in life. We come with needs and God responds by providing exactly what we require. There is an urgency expressed in this statement. Repent earnestly. You can almost hear the prophet John crying out to those who surround him in the desert, "Repent, for the kingdom of God has come near" (Matthew 3:2, NRSV). Indeed, that is the point. Whenever we acknowledge who we really are before God and seek reconciliation, God's reign breaks into our lives and peace can become a reality. The community is invited to confess "our sin" and we confess both before God and one another. None of this is private; all of this is intertwined and connected.

A communal act of confession immediately follows:

> Merciful God,
> we confess that we have not loved you with our whole heart.
> We have failed to be an obedient church.
> We have not done your will,
> we have broken your law,
> we have rebelled against your love,
> we have not loved our neighbors,
> and we have not heard the cry of the needy.
> Forgive us, we pray.
> Free us for joyful obedience,
> through Jesus Christ our Lord. Amen.[10]

Our failure to love constitutes our original and most grievous sin. St. Augustine described the basic problem of the fallen human being in terms of our disordered affections. Instead of loving God with the kind of wholehearted love that God deserves, we love ourselves in that way. If our loves were properly ordered, Augustine argued, we would love God as an end in Godself and love ourselves and others in such a way as to love God more fully. Because of the way we have twisted this around, all kinds of dysfunction and brokenness spill out of this distortion of our hearts. We fail to be the kind of community God intended. The

Prayer of Confession and Pardon, moreover, identifies the primary concern here in terms of disobedience. It is not that we don't know what God intends. No, we actually know that God calls us to be loving, merciful, compassionate, just, and true; but we choose to be something other than this. We embrace the ways of the world instead of the way and will of God.

The prayer then names specific practical areas of consistent failure. We follow our own devices and we break God's law, particularly the law of love which binds us inextricably both to God and to neighbor. We fail, in other words, at the most basic level—the two great commandments given to us in Scripture—to love God fully and to love our neighbors as we love ourselves (see Mark 12:30-31). We shut our ears and close our eyes to the many needs of others that surround us in life. Perhaps even worse, we have become callous toward and cynical about the suffering, disadvantaged, and marginal brothers and sisters of our human family. A period of silence often follows the recitation of this confession because it really does require that we ponder deeply just how far we have missed the mark in our common life.

The liturgy reflects the way in which the mandate to confess our sin is bound inextricably to God's promise of forgiveness. The structure of the liturgy itself reminds us of our need and God's action. So words of pardon follow immediately after the community has had time to ponder the concerns of the heart. The pastor proclaims to the people, "Hear the good news: Christ died for us while we were yet sinners; that proves God's love toward us. In the name of Jesus Christ, you are forgiven!" We know intuitively that we need to hear these words often. Paul Tillich, a great twentieth-century theologian, once claimed that the most difficult thing for any human being to do is accept the fact that she or he has been accepted by God. Even in this moment, let that sink in. "In the name of Jesus Christ, you are forgiven!" Your identity as a child of God resides in these words. The community celebrates that God has forgiven sin. Relationships have been restored. God's rule of justice and love has broken into the world anew, reclaiming and restoring the community of faith. Because of this, genuine peace is possible. Before the community moves to the table, it acknowledges that the goal of peace has been achieved by offering one another signs of reconciliation and love.

It is impossible to overestimate the value of these words and actions in terms of how the repetition of this pattern shapes the life of the church. Words shape us. Actions form us. And these words and actions represent one of the most fundamental aspects of our life together as God's children. We become what we say and what we do.

The Collect for Purity. Earlier in the Service of Word and Table, immediately following the opening hymn, the community prays together an ancient prayer known as the Collect for Purity. This prayer sets the tone for the Eucharistic action that consummates the service. I alluded to this collect in the opening pages of this volume in reference to the prayer of Steve Harper. In one voice, the church prays:

> Almighty God,
> to you all hearts are open, all desires known,
> and from you no secrets are hidden.
> Cleanse the thoughts of our hearts
> by the inspiration of your Holy Spirit,

that we may perfectly love you,
and worthily magnify your holy name,
through Christ our Lord. Amen.[11]

This prayer has been a constant part of the Eucharistic liturgy in the Anglican tradition since 1549 and may be found also in the current *United Methodist Book of Worship* and the *Hymnal*. David deSilva provides a magisterial examination of this prayer in his volume on *Sacramental Life*. He comes to the crux of this appeal to God in these powerful statements:

> This collect trains us to become increasingly aware of our transparency before God, for only thus can God make us transparent to ourselves. . . . [T]he collect teaches us an important dimension of the practice of the presence of God, the God who searches the heart and brings what is hidden—even from ourselves—to God's healing light. . . . [E]ven in the face of this discomfort, we can lower our defenses before God and his Word because we know that his desire is to free us from our divided heart for glad, single-hearted pursuit of new life in Christ.[12]

The General Confession. Thomas Cranmer prepared one of the most enduring prayers of confession since the time of the Reformation for inclusion in the 1552 *Book of Common Prayer*. On a pattern as ancient as the Sarum Breviary, restored by Cranmer, The General Confession has been prayed twice a day in the recitation of Morning and Evening Prayer. In his construction of these services of prayer, Cranmer drew on a number of medieval sources, including the Sarum rite. The General Confession reflects various penitential elements from Prime and Compline, one of the morning and one of the evening services of the Benedictine cycle of daily prayer. So while its form comes from the sixteenth century, its roots extend as far back as a millennium. The version of the General Confession that follows is the same form that John and Charles Wesley would have recited daily in the eighteenth century, a form prayed well into the twentieth century in the Methodist tradition.

> Almighty and most merciful Father,
> We have erred and strayed from thy ways like lost sheep.
> We have followed too much the devices and desires of our own hearts.
> We have offended against thy holy laws.
> We have left undone those things which we ought to have done;
> And we have done those things which we ought not to have done;
> And there is no health in us.
> But thou, O Lord, have mercy upon us, miserable offenders.
> Spare thou them, O God, which confess their faults.
> Restore thou them that are penitent;
> According to thy promises declared unto mankind in Christ Jesus our Lord.
> And grant, O most merciful Father, for his sake,
> That we may hereafter live a godly, righteous, and sober life;
> To the glory of thy holy Name. Amen.[13]

This prayer provides a comprehensive description of our universal sinful condition. In this regard it echoes the language of Isaiah 53:6: "All we like sheep have gone astray; / we have all turned to our own way" (NRSV). Our fixation on our own desires and way in the church rather than God's vision and will for harmonious living leads us to break God's law. Like sheep, we are a flock or community easily led along destructive paths that lead to death. We are convicted not only by what we have done—sins of commission—but also by what we have left undone—sins of omission. This prayer teaches us that "our sin is not to be measured in deeds alone," wrote John Stott, "but in the disease of our fallen nature."[14] This disease depletes our spiritual health. In the end, all the "miserable offender" can do is plead for mercy. The central cry of all these prayers of the gathered church, in fact, is the ancient supplication *Kyrie Eleison*—Lord, have mercy. In one voice from within the community of faith the penitents implore God not only to spare them, but also to restore them. Finally, this communal confession looks beyond the promised forgiveness to the formation of lives in which God restores all relationships, with God, with others, and with ourselves—lives that are godly, righteous, and sober. As Irenaeus maintained, "the greatest glory of God is the child of God fully alive."[15]

An Act of Repentance. Over the past twenty years The United Methodist Church has been engaged in various formal acts of repentance in response to its conviction about the continuing reality of racism in our world and the church's complicity with it. These acts of communal confession have taken place in public settings at the General Conference in the context of the worshiping community. Beginning in 2000, the first service of repentance specifically identified the sin of racism for which the church was responsible and asked the African Methodist denominations, in particular, for forgiveness. In 2004, A Service of Appreciation for Those Who Stayed was dedicated to the African-Americans who kept their membership within The United Methodist Church. Four years later,

Truth and Wholeness: Understanding White Privilege called white United Methodists to acknowledge their unearned privilege and seek to move beyond it into a more just future modeled after God's vision of shalom. Preparations for a 2012 General Conference Act of Repentance toward Healing Relationships with Indigenous People included listening sessions with indigenous peoples in Norway, the Philippines, and the United States.

Excerpts from the Litany of Reconciliation used as an act of repentance at the 2012 General Conference reflect the way in which the acknowledgment of our brokenness provides a foundation for our healing and the recovery of our proper vocation as God's people:

Bishop: The Gospel calls us to celebrate and protect the worth and dignity of all peoples. We acknowledge that we, as individuals and as a church, have not sufficiently confessed our lack of understanding, apathy, and sin. Confession of our guilt is a first step toward wholeness.

Delegates: Save us, O God, from the pride that is synonymous with death.

Bishop: In our desire to seek reconciliation with all people, we do not minimize our sin and complicity. We simply seek your Holy Spirit to fill us with a deep desire to support, assist, and reconcile with those who have not known or understood the native people within and outside the church. Foster a deep sense of community with all Native Americans.

Delegates: Lord, make our entire life a response to your invitation of Love; may each moment draw us closer to you and to each other.

Bishop: This is a time of new beginnings; to pray and to work for that new day in relationship with all peoples. The church is called through your mercy, O God, to become a channel of the reconciling Spirit of Jesus Christ and an instrument of love in the development of new relations. We affirm for the church and ourselves that many elements of our traditions and cultures are consistent with the gospel of Jesus Christ. We affirm that the Holy Spirit is faithful in guiding us in holy living. We invite the entire Church to receive the gifts of Native people as people of God.

Delegates: Lord, Jesus, freedom and truth prepares us for Eternal Life with you. Help us to cling only to the truth that brings about unfailing friendship with you. O God, you have given us the grace to be the instruments of love, and have commissioned us to proclaim forgiveness and condemnation; deliverance to the captive and captivity to the proud: Give us the patience of those who understand, and the impatience of those who love, that the might of your gentleness may work through us, and the mercy of your wrath may speak through us; in the name of Jesus Christ and for his sake. Amen.[16]

DIMENSIONS OF COMMUNAL SIN AND CONFESSION

All these prayers remind us how, in our communities of faith, we have failed in our witness to God's love in the world. We fail to be obedient to the calling God has given us, often manifesting attitudes of self-righteousness and judgmentalism, and need to repent of these signs of spiritual arrogance. A number of common themes run through these various prayers of communal confession, from the Prayer of Confession associated with the Eucharist to the Act of Repentance related to racism. First and foremost, we fail to love God. Our hearts are turned in on themselves and our lives characterized by self-interest, rather than being turned toward God and lived in self-sacrificial love toward others. We disobey God. We break God's laws and rebel against God's love. Rather than modeling a life of gratitude and benevolence, the community of faith grasps for power, prestige, and privilege in efforts to preserve and justify itself. We sin in "thought, word, and deed," but equally grieve God in our failure to take action in the direction of justice and peace in our broken world. Too often our common life is characterized by hypocrisy, exclusivity, divisiveness, and silence in the face of evil.

Ted Jennings provides this stinging indictment:

> We live in a culture that thrives on illusion, pretense, and masking. We participate all too willingly in these illusions. We live in a world that persuades itself that greater amounts of goods engender greater happiness, that more weapons mean more security, that it is our right to control the earth's resources, that human rights are luxuries, that justice is dispensed by the privileged and proud, that the end of communism (or capitalism) is the beginning of a new age, that the ends justify the means, that life is less important if it is clothed in skin of a different color or speaks a different tongue or worships in a different way. . . . Practice in confession is practice in penetrating illusion, in unmasking idols, in exposing pretense.[17]

Communal confession names these failures and opens the heart of the church to God's forgiving and restorative influence.

In his novel *Blue Like Jazz*, Donald Miller describes how one group of college students decided to respond to the challenge of a brokenness among God's people.[18] Facing a perception that Christians are too quick to judge, too eager to be right, and prone to exclude—with all of this confirmed, of course, by their classmates—they developed an idea. Their college held a renaissance festival every year that provided an opportunity for everyone to party and go wild. This small group thought this would be a perfect opportunity to let everyone know there were still a few Christians on campus. They decided to build a confession booth in the middle of campus and paint a sign on it that said "Confess your sins." When the group gathered together to talk about how this would work, one organizer explained, "Here's the catch. We are not actually going to accept confessions. We are going to confess to them. We are going to confess that, as followers of Jesus, we have not been very loving; we have been bitter, and for that we are sorry."

When the first student arrived, no one could hardly have anticipated what would happen. The thing is, those followers of Jesus really wanted to apologize for the many ways they had misrepresented the Lord. They felt that they had betrayed the Lord by judging, by not being willing to love the people he had loved. Those who came in a frivolous spirit "to confess" were completely surprised by the authenticity they encountered. After the Christians had delivered their confessions, many of those who came with the intention to sneer wanted to hug them when they were done. All those who visited the booth were grateful and gracious. All of them, on both sides, were changed through the process. These students were courageous to identify the sins in which they had been complicit in the community of faith.

From among the many sins of the church today, three seem to stand out in my mind: our captivity to fear, our silence in the face of injustice, and our penchant for division. I have found the vision of a seasoned church leader in South Africa, Peter Storey, and the prayers of a contemporary pilgrim, Barbara Hedges-Goettl, to be extremely compelling as I have reflected on these concerns. So their work will provide something of a backdrop to this discussion of fear, injustice, and division.

Fear. Various forms of the statement "do not be afraid" appear at least 365 times in the Bible. Some Christian spiritual writers have described fear as the eighth deadly sin—a particularly challenging area of brokenness for both individuals and communities. Fear menaces the church primarily because it stands in diametrical opposition to love. We fear what we do not know, and this fear creeps into the life of the church as well as the individual heart. "There is no fear in love, but perfect love casts out fear;" asserts the writer of 1 John, "and whoever fears has not reached perfection in love" (1 John 4:18, NRSV).

Fear is the root of all racism, bigotry, and exclusivism. In a sermon prior to the Soweto shootings in June 1976, Peter Storey uttered these prophetic words: "Racism is a disease of the heart; it is rooted in the fear that casts out love; it cannot be divorced from our selfishness and pride."[19] In 2004 the World Council of Churches engaged in a study of racism in the church and published its findings in a resource guide entitled *Transformative Justice: Being Church and Overcoming Racism*.[20] This significant document declares that racism is a sin because it denies the very source of humanity—the image of God in humankind—assumes that human beings are not equal before God and are not part of God's family, and separates us from God and from other human beings. The document confesses that churches are caught up in this sin and calls for the church to repent.

Martin Luther King, Jr. devoted his life and ministry to the exposure and eradication of racism and xenophobia in the life of the church. In *Where Do We Go from Here?* he describes the realities and consequences of this sin:

> Racism is a philosophy based on a contempt for life. It is the arrogant assertion that one race is the center of value and object of devotion, before which other races must kneel in submission. It is the absurd dogma that one race is responsible for all the progress of history and alone can assure the progress of the future. Racism is total estrangement. It separates not only bodies, but minds and spirits. Inevitably it descends to inflicting spiritual and physical homicide upon the out-group.[21]

Fear not only produces racism, it spawns all xenophobic attitudes and behaviors that separate us from "others." What a tragedy when the church succumbs to the temptations of this destructive trajectory instead of committing itself to God's vision of beloved community. You can see, therefore, how serious this particular sin is in the life of the church because it strikes at the very root of the Christian faith.

Barbara Hedges-Goettl's prayer confessing our captivity to fear invites us into a truthful acknowledgment of our failure in this regard:

CONFESSING OUR CAPTIVITY TO FEAR[22]

Call to Confession:

Although God has given the church the message of reconciliation in and through Jesus Christ, we fall short of God's call to be salt of the earth and light of the world:

Prayer (unison):

God, our fears and prejudices run deep. Sometimes we can only see our own point of view. We stick with those who are like us, rarely venturing outside our comfort zones. We do not hear those crying for justice and true peace. We blame those who are suffering and in need, instead of standing by them. We deny the power of your gospel to unite us with those who are different from us. Lord, give us eyes to see and ears to hear. Open us to new possibilities of life for all of your people, and use us to enact the new life given in Christ.

Assurance of Forgiveness

One: God's life-giving Word and Spirit conquer the powers of sin and death. Thanks be to God for the Good News:

All: In Jesus Christ, we are forgiven.

Injustice. In a typically incisive and prophetic examination of silence in the biblical witness, Walter Brueggemann illustrates how marginalized people break repressive silence and speak out against injustice.[23] He seeks to motivate readers to interrupt the silence so as not to be complicit with injustice in the worlds they inhabit. Too often the church has remained silent in the face of evil, injustice, and dehumanization. The gospel demands that the community of faith speak out, interrupting silence with its confession. In his presidential address to the South African Council of Churches in 1982, Peter Storey spoke of the injustice of apartheid as their struggle against this diabolical system was reaching its climax. The silence of many Christians in the face of this evil had been deafening and some Christians even continued to support the racist ideology and theology of apartheid.

In the face of silence and complicity, Storey broke the silence, celebrating God's rule and admonishing the faithful to live in God's future now: "In a world of cruelty we know that compassion and caring will one day rule—so we will demonstrate them *now*. . . . While this world bows to the love of power, we will cry, "No!"—we will live by the power of love *now*. While people live comfortably with injustice we know that justice will one day rule—it must therefore be our standard *now*."[24] He encouraged the followers of Jesus to stand boldly against the injustices of his day. Elsewhere he wrote that "we must faithfully hold before all our people God's unwavering dream of justice and *shalom*. Without that enduring vision on the horizon, calling us on and giving firm direction, we will soon be lost."[25]

Before we are able to live into this vision, we must repent the ways in which we have turned our backs on the way and will of God in our common life. Injustice continues to surround us at every turn and the church often remains silent in the face of it. While The United Methodist Church has a long history of concern for social justice, the "church writ large" and local congregations sometimes turn a deaf ear and a blind eye to pressing needs in their own communities. Silence is often the order of the day in relation to issues such as immigration reform and human rights, economic and environmental justice, the plight of women and children, homophobia and xenophobia, and the quest for peace with justice.

In *The Church for the World*, Jennifer McBride claims that, in addition to our work for justice, the church's act of public confession is one of the important ways in which we proclaim the gospel in the world. Based upon insights drawn from the work of the Lutheran martyr and theologian, Dietrich Bonhoeffer, McBride argues that "churches may courageously demonstrate Christ's redemptive work and offer a nontriumphal witness to the lordship of Christ when their mode of being in the world is confession of sin unto repentant action." She constructs a theology of public witness through the lens of communal confession "because confession and repentance directly correspond to the crucified Christ, whose form, Bonhoeffer argues, the church must take in order to be a faithful witness to the whole of Christ's person and work."[26] Barbara Hedges-Goettl invites us to break the silence and offer an act of repentance in the face of our complicity with injustice:

CONFESSING OUR SILENCE IN THE FACE OF INJUSTICE[27]

Call to Confession:

God calls the church to follow him, standing by those who suffer and are in need, so that justice may roll down like waters and righteousness like an ever-flowing stream. Let us confess the ways in which we do not follow God's call.

Prayer

One: O God, you bring justice to the oppressed and give bread to the hungry.

All: Forgive us when we do not follow you.

One: You free the prisoner and restore sight to the blind.

All: Forgive us when we do not follow you.

One: You support the downtrodden and protect the stranger.

All: Forgive us when we do not follow you.

One: You block evildoers and help orphans and widows.

All: Forgive us when we do not follow you.

One: You stand against injustice. You stand with the wronged.

All: Forgive us when we do not follow you.

One: You condemn those who seek their own interests, controlling and harming others.

All: Forgive us when we do not follow you.

One: You bring about justice and true peace among people.

All: God, forgive us when we do not follow you. Grant us your grace.

Embolden us that, as your people, we may stand where you stand.

Assurance of Forgiveness

One: God's life-giving Word and Spirit enable us to live in a new obedience, opening new possibilities of life for society and the world. Thanks be to God for the Good News:

All: In Jesus Christ, we are forgiven.

Division. Unfortunately, the Christian community is caught up frequently in the divisive spirit of this age and sometimes contributes to increased animosity and alienation by promoting a defective gospel, rather than living in and for God's vision of beloved community in this world. Instead of accepting our role as ambassadors of peace and reconciliation, those of us in the church sometimes foment division and use our power to "win" the battles we feel we must engage, often to the detriment of our mission. Peter Storey offers a prophetic word with regard to this kind of divisive spirit as well:

> If we are to be Christ's peacemakers, then we must learn his ways. The uniqueness of Jesus lay not only in what he said but in who he was and how he lived. In his life the congruence between word and deed was absolute, and because of that he could be the supreme peacemaker, breaking down the "dividing wall" that divides us from God and from each other (Ephesians 2:14). . . . In a world of cynicism, where the ugly and selfish dimensions of human nature are too often uppermost, there is something surprising and beautiful about a *living example of the difference.*[28]

All too often the church succumbs to the temptation of setting truth against love, of confusing a part of the truth for its whole, of confusing essentials with opinions, of embracing power as a weapon against others, of living in a posture of arrogance and self-righteousness instead of assuming the posture of servanthood and self-giving love. Instead of reaching out to all as beloved brothers and sisters in Christ, we too easily find solace in living life only with those who look and think like us. Speaking out of his own context, Peter Storey reminds us that "when we sing 'Come into my heart, Lord Jesus,' he says, *'Only if I can bring my friends.'*"[29]

The time in which we live is one of the most polarized eras in our common memory. Divisions within our world and in our nation are endemic. While division in the human family is nothing new, the animosity expressed and acted out in our common life today reveal fault lines that threaten to tear us apart; we feel this just as much in the church as in the world.

Different groups label each other and abuse each other. Each claims that their views related to Scripture are correct and that their opponents are all wrong. Peter Storey offers a somewhat humorous analogy in the face of this standoff mentality in the life of the church. "[We] are like two castaways on a desert island," he claims. "The one has the can of food, the other has the can opener—and each thinks that life depends on him alone! We should have nothing to do with this absurd and unbiblical debate."[30] We need to ask God to displace our hearts of war with hearts of peace.

In his high priestly prayer, recorded in John 17, Jesus prays for the unity of the church. We do well to read his words often:

> I ask not only on behalf of these, but also on behalf of those who will believe in me through their word, that they may all be one. As you, Father, are in me and I am in you, may they also be in us, so that the world may believe that you have sent me. The glory that you have given me I have given them, so that they may be one, as we are one, I in them and you in me, that they may become completely one, so that the world may know that you have sent me and have loved them even as you have loved me. (20-23, NRSV)

What an amazing opportunity we have to demonstrate the love of God to the world through the witness of our unity in the face of the myriad divisions that surround us in life. If we offer nothing other than the rancor, divisiveness, and animosity we see daily in the world, then what, in fact, do we have to offer that the world has not already mastered. In order to experience the kind of unity Christ offers the church, we must first confess our penchant for division and be healed of this sickness in our hearts:

CONFESSING OUR PENCHANT FOR DIVISION[31]

Invitation:

The gift and obligation of unity is given and commanded by God for the Christian church. Together we confess that the one worldwide community of believers is not united:

Prayer of Confession:

God, forgive us. Our communion is not always visible to the world. Sometimes we allow threats to unity to enter the church, making it hard to see that we are your community. We act as though we do not need each other. We do not always love one another. We do not know and bear one another's burdens. We fail to build each other up. We do not always give ourselves willingly and joyfully to one another. Forgive us, and strengthen us so that we may live in the unity that you grant us.

Assurance of Forgiveness

One: By Christ's work, we are reconciled and united with God and with one another. Thanks be to God for the Good News:

All: In Jesus Christ, we are forgiven. Amen.

Before turning to some practical exercises related to communal confession, permit me to leave you with a series of questions that strikes at the heart of our need to confess as individuals and as God's family. These are some of the questions that John Wesley posed to his followers as they laid the foundation stone of the City Road Chapel in London.

Do you bear witness to a religion of love?
Are you a lover of God and all people? . . .
Do you love, not in word or speech, but in truth and action?
Do you persevere in the work of faith and the labor of love?
Do you live in love, as Christ loved us and gave himself up for us?
Do you do good to every person as much and as often as you can?
If you do the will of my Father who is in heaven,
then you are my brother, and sister, and mother.
If your heart is the same as my heart in these things,
give me your hand.[32]

PRACTICE OF COMMUNAL CONFESSION

Collect for Purity or General Confession Exercise. In his book *Sacramental Life* David deSilva provides an exercise related to the Collect for Purity that I would like to adapt for our purposes here.[33] He suggests that you copy the words of the Collect for Purity onto a small card. I suggest that you could do this with the words of the General Confession as well. Read either of these communal confessions at the beginning of your day. You might even consider memorizing the prayers. Throughout the course of the day find moments in which to pray the prayer or even just a phrase of the prayer. Use these words to help bring you into or remind you of God's presence. Be as transparent before God as possible. Be attentive to the changes of your feelings or disposition that the Holy Spirit is working in you. Use your imagination to picture thousands upon thousands of Christians who have prayed these prayers through the centuries. Celebrate the sense of connection you feel to them in the movement from sin to redemption as you open yourself as a part of the church to God's forgiving presence. Carry these cards with you throughout the day and draw upon the power of these words as you experience temptation or spiritual distress.

Reflection on Worship Service. In an experience of worship in your local congregation or other setting of Christian worship, give focused attention to the way in which you are invited to confess sin. Is there, in fact, a time for communal confession and pardon? If yes, what are the particular concerns raised in this time of repentance and transformation? How do the words of the confession shape your vision of who you are and who God calls you to be? If no, ask yourself what effect the absence of confession has on your heart, mind, and soul. What feelings are stirred up in you as you reflect on the confession you have prayed? At the conclusion of the service write down one or two resolutions drawn out of your experience of confession and pardon. Ask yourself the questions, What is God calling me to do in light of this confession? What action must I take as a consequence of God's forgiveness in this dimension of our life with Christ? Commit yourself, then, under the guidance and by the power of the Holy Spirit, to act.

Creative Experiences of Communal Confession. If you are a pastor, consider providing your congregation an opportunity of creative communal confession. If you are a layperson, engage your pastor, or those responsible for worship, in conversation about such a creative experience. Sometimes it is really helpful to do something different or new in order to help yourself and others connect with communal confession in a helpful and relevant way. Here is just one example adapted from a resource known as SeasonsFUSION.[34]

Station four readers in the four corners of your worship space. Provide each of them with the three lists of words below with four words each—all words of confession. Instruct the readers to take turns saying one of the words from each of the lists in order around the sanctuary. Also suggest that they give ample pause between each of the words to provide the congregation time for silent reflection.

The pastor or liturgist introduces the experience by saying: "May these words remind us of our need to repent and to ask for God's forgiveness." The readers then speak the following words:

- separation, division, prejudice, exclusion;
- harm, neglect, pollution, extinction;
- disregard, ignore, injustice, impoverish.

After all the words have been read, the pastor or liturgist offers a time of silent reflection, after an appropriate amount of time, saying: "Hear now these life-giving words: May these words take root within us and become the living reality among and through us."

Have the same four readers then read the following words of affirmation in the same way they read the previous lists, but without any space between each word.

- forgiven, forgiven, forgiven, forgiven;
- receive, welcome, reconcile, enfold;
- restore, conserve, beautify, care;
- listen, share, compassion, love.

The pastor or liturgist concludes with the words: "In the name of Jesus Christ, we are all a forgiven and reconciled people." The congregation responds: "Thanks be to God."

Acts of Public Repentance. Reach out to a specific group of people in the life of your community that you feel you have wronged in some way through racist or xenophobic attitudes and actions. For example, if you are a white pastor, connect with an African-American, Hispanic/Latino, or Native/Indigenous pastor and express your desire to develop an act of public repentance with them in which you acknowledge your sin and seek reconciliation. Notice who your neighbors are. Learn their stories. If possible, reach beyond the context of the Christian community to those who practice other religions as well (Muslims, Jews, Hindus, and others) or the LGBTQ+ community, developing an act of repentance and reconciliation in conjunction with their leaders. You know the forms of racism and xenophobia that have damaged relationships in your own context, so explore ways to reach across these divides in the hope of bringing peace and healing to your community.

Questions for Personal Reflection and Group Discussion

1. What practices of communal confession have you participated in? Which are common in your worshiping community? Find a recent order of worship and review your church's practice. Which communal prayers of confession shared in the text have you experienced? How did they or did they not resonate in your life and community?

2. If your church set up a confession booth, what sins would it need to confess to your community?

For what and to whom would other communities you're a part of need to confess?

3. Consider the three identified dimensions of communal sin and confession (pages 109–121). For what fears and results of fears does your community need to confess? For what injustices and results of injustices does your community need to confess? For what division and results of division does your community need to confess? If you are part of a worshiping community, consider using or offering one or more of the suggested confessions to be used in your worship.

4. If you are studying this text with a small group, identify a leader and participate in one of the provided confessions from this chapter as a group.

5. Go back to page 121 and review the section "Practice of Communal Confession." If you have not already done so, identify one suggested activity in which you will participate.

EPILOGUE

The practice of confession is just one among many spiritual practices that can help you deepen your relationship with the triune God and your brothers and sisters in the human family. As one of the great desert fathers, Dorotheos of Gaza, observed, we are like the spokes of a wheel, and the closer we come to God, who is the hub, the closer we come to one another. All the various forms of confession—confession of faith and individual sins, mutual, and communal confession—enable us to love God more fully and to love our neighbors as ourselves. Confession, more than anything else, is an invitation into a lifelong journey characterized by personal and communal repentance, spiritual transformation, and freedom to love.

To practice confession means to participate in God's great work of new creation. This spiritual exercise tunes your heart to the keynote of love. It has the ability to liberate your spirit as it experiences the movements of mourning, listening, prostrating, and ultimately standing before God and one another as the beautiful child of God you have been created to be. Confession is all about freedom—freedom from sin and freedom to love. I close with these words of encouragement from an early Methodist woman, Grace Murray, who rejoiced in this very discovery for herself:

> I was filled with light and love. I saw my lost estate in Adam and my recovery by Christ Jesus. My soul was overpowered and I cried out to those that were with me, "If all the devils in hell were dancing round me, I fear them not." I was as sensible, when the guilt of sin was removed from my conscience, as a man pressed under a load is sensible when it is taken off his shoulders. Now, therefore, God having set my soul at liberty, he opened my lips to praise him.[1]

Confession liberates the soul. Confession opens a pathway to reconciliation and restoration. Confession helps us sing the song of love. Join the chorus!

WORKS CITED

"America's Four Gods." In *American Piety in the 21st Century: New Insights to the Depth and Complexity of Religion in the US,* Baylor University Institute for Studies in Religion, Selected Findings from the Baylor Religion Survey, September 2006. https://www.baylor.edu/baylorreligionsurvey/doc.php/288937.pdf; accessed December 20, 2018.

Appleton, George, ed. *The Oxford Book of Prayer.* New York: Oxford University Press, 1985.

Bonhoeffer, Dietrich. *Life Together.* New York: Harper & Row, 1954.

The Book of Common Prayer. New York: Oxford University Press, 1928.

Brianchaninov, Ignatius. *On the Prayer of Jesus.* London: New Seeds Books, 2006.

Brueggemann, Walter. *Interrupting Silence: God's Command to Speak Out.* Louisville: Westminster John Knox Press, 2018.

Bruner, Jason. "Contesting Confession in the East African Revival." *Anglican and Episcopal History* 84, 3 (September 2015): 253-78.

Bruner, Jason. *Living Salvation in the East African Revival in Uganda.* Rochester: University of Rochester Press, 2017.

Bruner, Jason. "Public Confession and the Moral Universe of the East African Revival." *Studies in World Christianity* 18, 3 (November 2012): 254-268.

Calvin, John. I*nstitutes of the Christian Religion.* Edited by John T. McNeill. 2 vols. Philadelphia: Westminster Press, 1960.

Chilcote, Paul W. "'All the Image of Thy Love': Charles Wesley's Vision of the One Thing Needful," *Proceedings of The Charles Wesley Society* 18 (2014): 21-40.

Chilcote, Paul W. *Changed from Glory into Glory: Wesleyan Prayer for Transformation.* Nashville: Upper Room Books, 2005.

Chilcote, Paul W. *Early Methodist Spirituality: Selected Women's Writings.* Nashville: Kingswood Books, 2007.

Chilcote, Paul W. *The Imitation of Christ: Selections Annotated & Explained.* Woodstock, VT: SkyLight Paths, 2012.

Chilcote, Paul W. *Praying in the Wesleyan Spirit: 52 Lessons for Today* (Nashville: Upper Room Books, 2001.

Chilcote, Paul W. *The Wesleyan Tradition: A Paradigm for Renewal.* Nashville: Abingdon Press, 2002.

Clarke, Adam. *Clarke's Commentary: The Holy Bible Containing the Old and New Testaments with a Commentary and Critical Notes.* Ralph Earle, abr. 6 vols. London: Ward, Lock, & Co, 1881.

Clebsch, William A. and Charles R. Jaekle. *Pastoral Care in Historical Perspective.* New York: Harper & Row, 1964.

Compiani, Maurizio. *Confession: The Sacrament of Mercy.* Huntington, IN: Pontifical Council for the Promotion of the New Evangelization, 2015.

Davies, B. and G. R. Evans, eds., *Anselm of Canterbury—The Major Works*. Oxford: Oxford University Press, 1998. *(Cur Deus Homo)*

Deatherage, Dane. "Mutual Confession: A Holy Experiment," The Gospel Coalition, September 24, 2014; https://www.thegospelcoalition.org/article/mutual-confession-a-holy-experiment/; accessed January 24, 2019.

deSilva, David A. *Sacramental Life: Spiritual Formation Through the Book of Common Prayer.* Downers Grove, IL: IVP Books, 2008.

de Waal, Esther. *A Life-giving Way: A Commentary on the Rule of St. Benedict.* Collegeville, MN: The Liturgical Press, 1995.

Drury, Amanda Hontz. *Saying Is Believing: The Necessity of Testimony in Adolescent Spiritual Development.* Downers Grove, IL: InterVarsity Press, 2015.

Finney, Charles Grandison. "Mutual Confession of Faults, and Mutual Prayer." *The Oberlin Evangelist*, January 17, 1849. https://www.whatsaiththescripture.com/Voice/Oberlin_1849/OE1849.Confession.Prayer.html; accessed January 24, 2019.

Forest, Jim. *Confession: Doorway to Forgiveness.* Maryknoll, NY: Orbis Books, 2002.

Foster, Richard J. *Celebration of Discipline: The Path to Spiritual Growth.* New York: HarperCollins Publishers, 1978.

Foster, Richard J. *Prayer: Finding the Heart's True Home.* New York: HarperSanFrancisco, 1992.

Gateley, Edwina. *I Hear A Seed Growing: God of the Forest, God of the Streets.* 20th anniversary edition. Orbis Books, 2011.

Gododo-Madikileza, Pumla. "Remorse, Forgiveness, and Rehumanization: Stories from South Africa." *Journal of Humanistic Psychology* 42, 1 (Winter 2002): 7-32.

Hahn, Scott. *Lord, Have Mercy: The Healing Power of Confession.* New York: Doubleday, 2003.

Hedges-Goettl, Barbara. *Prayers.* http://oga.pcusa.org/site_media/media/uploads/oga/pdf/worship_liturgy_web.pdf.

Jennings, Theodore W., Jr. *The Liturgy of Liberation: The Confession and Forgiveness of Sins.* Nashville: Abingdon Press, 1988.

Johnson, Ben Campbell. *Invitation to Pray.* Decatur, GA: CTS Press, 1992.

Kaiser, Joshua A. *Becoming Simple and Wise: Moral Discernment in Dietrich Bonhoeffer's Vision of Christian Ethics.* Eugene, OR: Pickwick Publications, 2015.

King, Martin Luther King, Jr. *Where Do We Go from Here: Chaos or Community?* Boston: Beacon Press, 1967.

Lapsley, Jacqueline E., et al. *Women's Bible Commentary.* 3rd ed. Louisville: Westminster John Knox Press, 2012.

Larson, Catherine Claire. *As We Forgive: Stories of Reconciliation from Rwanda.* Grand Rapids: Zondervan, 2009.

Lewis, C. S. *The Magician's Nephew, The Chronicles of Narnia Book 1.* New York: Harper Collins, 2008.

"Litany of Reconciliation," 2012 General Conference Act of Repentance toward Healing Relationships with Indigenous People. http://s3.amazonaws.com/content.newsok.com/documents/Litany%20of%20Reconciliation.pdf; accessed January 20, 2019.

Luther, Martin. "A Simple Way to Pray," in *Luther's Works.* Edited by Gustav K. Wiencke. Philadelphia: Fortress Press, 1968.

Mbiti, John. "Peace and Reconciliation in African Religion," *Dialogue & Alliance: Peacebuilding in Africa 24*, 1 (Spring/Summer 2010): np.

McBride, Jennifer M. *The Church for the World: A Theology of Public Witness.* New York: Oxford University Press, 2012.

McNeill, John T. *A History of the Cure of Souls.* New York: Harper & Brothers, 1951.

Miller, Donald. *Blue Like Jazz.* Nashville: Thomas Nelson, 2003.

Noffke, Suzanne, trans., *Catherine of Siena: The Dialogue.* Wahwah, NY: Paulist Press, 1980.

Nouwen, Henri J. M. *The Return of the Prodigal Son: A Story of Homecoming.* New York: Doubleday, 1992.

Pinnock, Clark K. & Robert C. Brow. *Unbounded Love: A Good News Theology for the 21st Century.* Eugene, OR; Wipf and Stock Publishers, 2000.

Pope Francis. General Audience of February 19, 2014. http://w2.vatican.va/content/francesco/en/audiences/2014/documents/papa-francesco_20140219_udienza-generale.html; accessed November 14, 2018.

Pope Francis. *The Name of God Is Mercy: A Conversation with Andrea Tornielli.* Translated by Oonagh Stransky. New York: Random House, 2016.

"Roman Catholic Prayers of Confession;" http://www.preces-latinae.org/thesaurus/Confessio/ActusCont.html; accessed November 18, 2018.

St. Benedict, *The Rule.* Edited by Timothy Fry. Collegeville, MN: The Liturgical Press, 1980.

Schmemann, Alexander. "Some Reflections on Confession." Paper discussed at the Alumni Retreat, St. Andrew's Camp, June 20-22, 1961. http://www.schmemann.org/byhim/reflection-sonconfession.html; accessed November 15, 2018.

Simon, George, Jr. "How to Recognize True (and false) Contrition." A Cry for Justice blog, March 4, 2013. https://cryingoutforjustice.com/2013/03/04/how-to-recognize-true-and-false-contrition-by-dr-george-simon-jr/; accessed November 16, 2018.

Steere, Douglas. *On Beginning from Within.* New York: Harper & Brothers, 1943.

Stevenson, J., ed. *A New Eusebius.* London: SPCK, 1975. (Irenaeus, *Against Heresies*)

Stevenson, Robert Lewis. *Across the Plains with Other Memories and Essays.* New York: Charles Scribner's Sons, 1892.

Stewart, Columba. *Prayer and Community: The Benedictine Tradition.* Maryknoll, NY: Orbis Books, 1998.

Storey, Peter. *With God in the Crucible: Preaching Costly Discipleship.* Nashville: Abingdon Press, 2002.

Stott, John R. W. *Confess Your Sins: The Way of Reconciliation.* Philadelphia: Westminster Press, 1964.

Tamez, Elsa. *The Scandalous Message of James: Faith Without Works Is Dead.* New York: Crossroad Publishing Company, 1990.

Thompson, Marjorie J. *Soul Feast: An Invitation to the Christian Spiritual Life.* Louisville: Westminster John Knox Press, 1995.

Thomson, Robert W., ed. *Athanasius: Contra Genies and De Incarnatione.* Oxford: Clarendon Press, 1971. (Athanasius, *On the Incarnation*)

Transformative Justice: Being Church and Overcoming Racism, Resource Guide. Geneva: World Council of Churches, 2004.

The United Methodist Hymnal. Nashville: The United Methodist Publishing House, 1989.

"Twelve Steps of Alcoholics Anonymous, The." https://www.aa.org/assets/en_US/smf-121_en.pdf. Accessed July 29, 2019.

Wainwright, Geoffrey. *Doxology: The Praise of God in Worship, Doctrine, and Life.* New York: Oxford University Press, 1980.

Watson, David Lowes. *Accountable Discipleship: Handbook for Covenant Discipleship Groups in the Congregation.* Nashville: Discipleship Resources, 1985.

Watson, Kevin M. *Pursuing Social Holiness: The Band Meeting in Wesley's Thought and Popular Methodist Practice.* Oxford: Oxford University Press, 2014.

Wesley, Charles. *Hymns for Those that Seek and Those that have Redemption in the Blood of Jesus Christ.* London: Strahan, 1747.

Wesley, Charles. *Short Hymns on Select Passages of the Holy Scriptures.* 2 vols. Bristol: Farley, 1762.

Wesley, John. *Sunday Service of the Methodists in North America.* Nashville: The United Methodist Publishing House, 1984.

Wesley, John. *The Works of John Wesley, Volume 2, Sermons II, 34-70.* Edited by Albert C. Outler. Nashville: Abingdon Press, 1985.

Wesley, John. *The Works of John Wesley, Volume 3, Sermons III, 71-114.* Edited by Albert C. Outler. Nashville: Abingdon Press, 1986.

Wesley, John. *The Works of John Wesley, Volume 9, The Methodist Societies.* Edited by Rupert E. Davies. Nashville: Abingdon Press, 1989.

Wilkinson, David. *Science, Religion, and the Search for Extraterrestrial Intelligence.* Oxford: Oxford University Press, 2013.

Willard, Dallas. *The Spirit of the Disciplines: Understanding How God Changes Lives.* New York: HarperSanFrancisco, 1988.

NOTES

CHAPTER ONE

[1] "America's Four Gods," in *American Piety in the 21st Century: New Insights to the Depth and Complexity of Religion in the US*, Baylor University Institute for Studies in Religion, Selected Findings from the Baylor Religion Survey, September 2006; https://www.baylor.edu/baylorreligionsurvey/doc.php/288937.pdf; accessed December 20, 2018.
[2] Clark K. Pinnock & Robert C. Brow, *Unbounded Love: A Good News Theology for the 21st Century* (Eugene, OR; Wipf & Stock, 2000).
[3] Pinnock & Brow, *Unbounded Love*, 8-9.
[4] *The United Methodist Hymnal* (Nashville: The United Methodist Publishing House, 1989), 877.
[5] Pinnock & Brow, *Unbounded Love,* 12.
[6] Charles Wesley, *Short Hymns on Select Passages of the Holy Scriptures*, 2 vols. (Bristol: Farley, 1762), 1:53-54, Hymns 169-71. All hymn texts are taken from Charles Wesley's Published Verse, Duke Center for Studies in the Wesleyan Tradition, https://divinity.duke.edu/initiatives-centers/cswt/wesley-texts, with grateful acknowledgment.
[7] See David Wilkinson, *Science, Religion, and the Search for Extraterrestrial Intelligence* (Oxford: Oxford University Press, 2013), 136.
[8] C. S. Lewis, *The Magician's Nephew: The Chronicles of Narnia, Book 1* (New York: HarperCollins Publishers, 2008), 106.
[9] John Wesley, *The Works of John Wesley, Volume 3, Sermons III, 71-114*, ed. Albert C. Outler (Nashville: Abingdon Press, 1986), 199-209.
[10] Athanasius, *On the Incarnation of the Word*, Chapter 54, Christian Classics Ethereal Library, https://www.ccel.org/ccel/athanasius/incarnation.ix.html; accessed August 19, 2019.
[11] See Paul W. Chilcote, "'All the Image of Thy Love': Charles Wesley's Vision of the One Thing Needful," *Proceedings of The Charles Wesley Society* 18 (2014): 21-40.
[12] Amanda Hontz Drury, *Saying Is Believing: The Necessity of Testimony in Adolescent Spiritual Development* (Downers Grove, IL: InterVarsity Press, 2015).
[13] Irenaeus, *Against Heresies*, I.2, in *A New Eusebius*, ed. J. Stevenson (London: SPCK, 1975), 115.
[14] Geoffrey Wainwright, *Doxology: The Praise of God in Worship, Doctrine, and Life: A Systematic Theology* (New York: Oxford University Press, 1980), 39-40.
[15] *The United Methodist Hymnal*, 35.
[16] Wainwright, *Doxology,* 183.
[17] Wainwright, *Doxology*, 183. See Wainwright's magisterial examination of the functions of creeds and hymns in Christian worship, pages 182-217.
[18] *The Book of Common Prayer* (New York: Oxford University Press, 1928), 95-96.
[19] Paul W. Chilcote, *The Wesleyan Tradition: A Paradigm for Renewal* (Nashville: Abingdon Press, 2002), 19-21.
[20] Pope Francis, *The Name of God Is Mercy: A Conversation with Andrea Tornielli*, trans. Oonagh Stransky (New York: Random House, 2016), 23.
[21] Martin Luther, "A Simple Way to Pray," in *Luther's Works*, ed. Gustav K. Wiencke (Philadelphia: Fortress Press, 1968), 200-201.

CHAPTER TWO

[1] Dietrich Bonhoeffer, *Life Together: The Classic Exploration of Christian Community* (New York: Harper & Row, 1954), 110.
[2] Charles Wesley, "Happy Magdalene," in *Hymns for Those that Seek and Those that have Redemption in the Blood of Jesus Christ* (London: Strahan, 1747), 12-13. Modernized spelling.
[3] Anselm, *Cur Deus Homo*, I.21, in B. Davies and G. R. Evans, eds., *Anselm of Canterbury—The Major Works* (Oxford: Oxford University Press, 1998), 305.

[4] For the video and full text of the Audience, see http://w2.vatican.va/content/francesco/en/audiences/2014/documents/papa-francesco_20140219_udienza-generale.html; accessed November 14, 2018.
[5] See my discussion of the parable in *Changed from Glory into Glory: Wesleyan Prayer for Transformation* (Nashville: Upper Room Books, 2005), 60-61, upon which this material is based.
[6] Jim Forest, *Confession: Doorway to Forgiveness* (Maryknoll, NY: Orbis Books, 2002), 49.
[7] Maurizio Compiani for the Pontifical Council for the Promotion of the New Evangelization, *Confession: The Sacrament of Mercy* (Huntington, IN: Our Sunday Visitor Publishing Division, 2015), 27.
[8] Henri J. M. Nouwen, *The Return of the Prodigal Son: A Story of Homecoming* (New York: Doubleday, 1992), 44.
[9] Richard Foster, *Celebration of Discipline: The Path to Spiritual Growth* (New York: HarperCollins Publishers, 1978), 151.
[10] Alexander Schmemann, "Some Reflections on Confession," Paper discussed at the Alumni Retreat, St. Andrew's Camp, June 20-22, 1961; http://www.schmemann.org/byhim/reflectionsonconfession.html; accessed November 15, 2018.
[11] Paul W. Chilcote, *The Imitation of Christ: Selections Annotated & Explained* (Woodstock, VT: SkyLight Paths, 2012), 153.
[12] Douglas V. Steere, *On Beginning from Within: On Listening to Another* (New York: Harper & Brothers, 1943), 80.
[13] Marjorie J. Thompson, *Soul Feast: An Invitation to the Christian Spiritual Life, New Revised Edition* (Louisville: Westminster John Knox Press, 2014), 97.
[14] Thompson, *Soul Feast*, 98; see also "The Twelve Steps of Alcoholics Anonymous," https://www.aa.org/assets/en_US/smf-121_en.pdf; accessed July 29, 2019.
[15] Thompson, *Soul Feast*, 98.
[16] Thompson, *Soul Feast*, 98-99.
[17] Forest, *Confession*, 94.
[18] Cited in Forest, *Confession*, 111.
[19] Chilcote, *The Imitation of Christ*, 149.
[20] Dr. George Simon, Jr., "How to Recognize True (and false) Contrition," A Cry for Justice blog, March 4, 2013, https://cryingoutforjustice.com/2013/03/04/how-to-recognize-true-and-false-contrition-by-dr-george-simon-jr/; accessed November 16, 2018.
[21] Pumla Gododo-Madikileza, "Remorse, Forgiveness, and Rehumanization: Stories from South Africa," *Journal of Humanistic Psychology* 42, 1 (Winter 2002): 7-32.
[22] Forest, *Confession*, 131.
[23] Forest, *Confession*, 136.
[24] Pope Francis, *The Name of God Is Mercy*, 22-23.
[25] Scott Hahn, *Lord, Have Mercy: The Healing Power of Confession* (New York: Doubleday, 2003), 91-102.
[26] Hahn, *Lord, Have Mercy*, 102.
[27] Compiani, *Confession*, 72.
[28] Foster, *Celebration of Discipline*, 146-47.
[29] Foster, *Celebration of Discipline*, 147.
[30] Foster, *Celebration of Discipline*, 148-49.
[31] Cited in Pope Francis, *The Name of God Is Mercy*, 132-34.
[32] Bonhoeffer, *Life Together*, 116.
[33] For the original Latin and this standard translation, see http://www.preces-latinae.org/thesaurus/Confessio/ActusCont.html; accessed November 18, 2018.
[34] For a full discussion of this simple and ancient prayer, see Ignatius Brianchaninov, *On the Prayer of Jesus* (London: New Seeds Books, 2006), xxiii–xxiv.
[35] Composed by the author.
[36] Paul W. Chilcote, *Praying in the Wesleyan Spirit: 52 Prayers for Today* (Nashville: Upper Room Books, 2001), 47-48.

[37] Author's summarization of the practice developed by Ignatius Loyola in his *Spiritual Practices*.
[38] Suzanne Noffke, trans., *Catherine of Siena: The Dialogue* (Wahwah, NY: Paulist Press, 1980), 364-366.
[39] Forest, *Confession*, 116-29.
[40] Forest, *Confession*, 129.

CHAPTER THREE
[1] Dallas Willard, *The Spirit of the Disciplines: Understanding How God Changes Lives* (New York: HarperSanFrancisco, 1988), 187-88.
[2] Catherine Claire Larson, *As We Forgive: Stories of Reconciliation from Rwanda* (Grand Rapids: Zondervan, 2009), 87.
[3] Larson, *As We Forgive*, 92.
[4] Robert Lewis Stevenson, "A Christmas Sermon, IV," *Across the Plains with Other Memories and Essays*; first published by Charles Scribner's Sons, 1892 (CreateSpace Independent Publishing Platform, 2017), 99.
[5] Quotation from personal conversation with John Mbiti. See also John Mbiti, "Peace and Reconciliation in African Religion," *Dialogue & Alliance: Peacebuilding in Africa* 24, 1 (Spring/Summer 2010); online journal: http://www.upf.org/resources/speeches-and-articles/3226-js-mbiti-peace-and-reconciliation-in-african-religion; accessed January 23, 2019.
[6] William A. Clebsch and Charles R. Jaekle, *Pastoral Care in Historical Perspective* (New York: Harper & Row, 1964), 95.
[7] John T. McNeill, *A History of the Cure of Souls* (New York: Harper & Brothers, 1951), 92.
[8] Pope Francis, *The Name of God Is Mercy*, 22.
[9] Bonhoeffer, *Life Together*, 114. I have changed Bonhoeffer's gendered language throughout this quotation so as to be fully inclusive.
[10] John Calvin, *Institutes of the Christian Religion*, ed. John T. McNeill, 2 vols. (Philadelphia: Westminster Press, 1960), 629 (III.4.6).
[11] Adam Clarke's *Commentary on the Bible*, Ralph Earle, abr., World Publishing (Kansas City: Beacon Hill Press, 1967), 1299 (James 5:16).
[12] Charles Grandison Finney, "Mutual Confession of Faults, and Mutual Prayer," *The Oberlin Evangelist*, January 17, 1849; https://www.whatsaiththescripture.com/Voice/Oberlin_1849/OE1849.Confession.Prayer.html; accessed January 24, 2019.
[13] Gay L. Byron, "James," in Jacqueline E. Lapsley, et al. *Women's Bible Commentary*. 3rd ed. (Louisville: Westminster John Knox Press, 2012), 615.
[14] Elsa Tamez, *The Scandalous Message of James: Faith Without Works Is Dead* (New York: Crossroad Publishing Company, 1990), 58.
[15] Dane Deatherage, "Mutual Confession: A Holy Experiment," The Gospel Coalition, September 24, 2014; https://www.thegospelcoalition.org/article/mutual-confession-a-holy-experiment/; accessed January 24, 2019.
[16] Author's paraphrase of end of chapter 72 of St. Benedict, *The Rule*, ed. Timothy Fry (Collegeville, MN: The Liturgical Press, 1980), 95.
[17] Columba Stewart, *Prayer and Community: The Benedictine Tradition* (Maryknoll, NY: Orbis Books 1998), 48.
[18] Esther de Waal, *A Life-giving Way: A Commentary on the Rule of St. Benedict* (Collegeville, MN: The Liturgical Press, 1995), 105.
[19] Stewart, *Prayer and Community*, 102.
[20] Stewart, *Prayer and Community*, 53.
[21] St. Benedict, *The Rule*, 66-67.
[22] de Waal, *A Life-giving Way*, 149-50.
[23] John Wesley, "A Plain Account of the People Called Methodists," VI.6, in John Wesley, *The Works of John Wesley, Volume 9, The Methodist Societies*, ed. Rupert E. Davies (Nashville: Abingdon Press, 1989), 268.

[24] John Wesley, "The Scripture Way of Salvation," I.8, *The Works of John Wesley, Volume 2, Sermons II, 34-70*, ed. Albert C. Outler (Nashville: Abingdon Press, 1985), 2:160.
[26] John Wesley, "Rules of the Band Societies" Wesley, *Works* 9:78.
[26] John Wesley, "Rules of the Band Societies" Wesley, *Works* 9:77-78.
[27] John Wesley, "Rules of the Band Societies" Wesley, *Works* 9:78.
[28] David Lowes Watson, *Accountable Discipleship: Handbook for Covenant Discipleship Groups in the Congregation* (Nashville: Discipleship Resources, 1985), 29.
[29] Cited in Kevin M. Watson, *Pursuing Social Holiness: The Band Meeting in Wesley's Thought and Popular Methodist Practice* (Oxford: Oxford University Press, 2014), 123.
[30] Watson, *Pursuing Social Holiness*, 66.
[31] Jason Bruner, "Public Confession and the Moral Universe of the East African Revival," *Studies in World Christianity* 18, 3 (November 2012): 254-268.
[32] Jason Bruner, "Contesting Confession in the East African Revival," *Anglican and Episcopal History* 84, 3 (September 2015): 259.
[33] Jason Bruner, *Living Salvation in the East African Revival in Uganda* (Rochester: University of Rochester Press, 2017).
[34] Bruner, "Contesting Confession," 262.
[35] Joshua A. Kaiser, *Becoming Simple and Wise: Moral Discernment in Dietrich Bonhoeffer's Vision of Christian Ethics* (Eugene, OR: Pickwick Publications, 2015), 111.
[36] Kaiser, *Becoming Simple and Wise*, 112.
[37] Kaiser, *Becoming Simple and Wise*, 112.
[38] Chilcote, *Praying in the Wesleyan Spirit*, 149-50.
[39] George Appleton, ed., *The Oxford Book of Prayer* (New York: Oxford University Press, 1985), 145.
[40] Ben Campbell Johnson, *Invitation to Pray* (Decatur, GA: CTS Press, 1992), 18-22 in particular.
[41] For information on the Ekklesia Project, consult http://www.ekklesiaproject.org/about-us/who-we-are/. The full study guide may be located at https://www.bethelcupertino.org/adults/2014_Fun_With_Faith/Dale-Ziemer-Life-Together-PDF.pdf; accessed January 25, 2019.
[42] For guidance on the development of Covenant Discipleship Groups, consult https://www.umcdiscipleship.org/resources/covenant-discipleship-groups-an-introduction, from which these suggestions are drawn.

CHAPTER FOUR
[1] David A. deSilva, *Sacramental Life: Spiritual Formation Through the Book of Common Prayer* (Downers Grove, IL: IVP Books, 2008), 109.
[2] Theodore W. Jennings, Jr., *The Liturgy of Liberation: The Confession and Forgiveness of Sins* (Nashville: Abingdon Press, 1988), 66-67.
[3] Compiani, *Confession*, 72-75.
[4] Compiani, *Confession*, 72.
[5] Edwina Gateley, *I Hear A Seed Growing: God of the Forest, God of the Streets*, 20th anniversary edition (Orbis Books, 2011), 61.
[6] Richard J. Foster, *Prayer: Finding the Heart's True Home* (New York: HarperSanFrancisco, 1992), 107-108.
[7] Jennings, *The Liturgy of Liberation*, 53.
[8] *The United Methodist Hymnal*, 6-31. Several different settings of the Service of Word and Table are delineated in this resource.
[9] *The United Methodist Hymnal*, 7.
[10] *The United Methodist Hymnal*, 8.
[11] *The United Methodist Hymnal*, 6.
[12] deSilva, *Sacramental Life*, 97.
[13] John Wesley, *Sunday Service of the Methodists in North America* (Nashville: The United Methodist Publishing House, 1984), 8.

[14] John R. W. Stott, *Confess Your Sins: The Way of Reconciliation* (Philadelphia: Westminster Press, 1964), 38.
[15] Irenaeus, *Against Heresies*, IV.20.7; author's own translation.
[16] "Litany of Reconciliation," 2012 General Conference Act of Repentance toward Healing Relationships with Indigenous People; http://s3.amazonaws.com/content.newsok.com/documents /Litany%20of%20Reconciliation.pdf; accessed January 20, 2019.
[17] Jennings, *Liturgy of Liberation*, 73-74.
[18] Donald Miller, *Blue Like Jazz: Nonreligious Thoughts on Christian Spirituality* (Nashville: Thomas Nelson, 2003), 116-27.
[19] Peter Storey, *With God in the Crucible: Preaching Costly Discipleship* (Nashville: Abingdon Press, 2002), 31.
[20] *Transformative Justice: Being Church and Overcoming Racism, Resource Guide* (Geneva: World Council of Churches, 2004).
[21] Martin Luther King, Jr., *Where Do We Go from Here: Chaos or Community?* (Boston: Beacon Press, 1967), 67.
[22] Barbara Hedges-Goettl. Used with permission. http://oga.pcusa.org/site_media/media /uploads/oga/pdf/worship_liturgy_web.pdf; accessed July 31, 2019.
[23] Walter Brueggemann, *Interrupting Silence: God's Command to Speak Out* (Louisville: Westminster John Knox Press, 2018).
[24] Storey, *With God in the Crucible*, 54.
[25] Storey, *With God in the Crucible*, 142.
[26] Jennifer M. McBride, *The Church for the World: A Theology of Public Witness* (New York: Oxford University Press, 2012), 11.
[27] Barbara Hedges-Goettl. Used with permission. http://oga.pcusa.org/site_media/media /uploads/oga/pdf/worship_liturgy_web.pdf; accessed July 31,2019.
[28] Storey, *With God in the Crucible*, 31.
[29] Storey, *With God in the Crucible*, 67.
[30] Storey, *With God in the Crucible*, 153.
[31] Barbara Hedges-Goettl. Used with permission. http://oga.pcusa.org/site_media/media /uploads/oga/pdf/worship_liturgy_web.pdf; accessed July 31, 2019.
[32] Wesley, *Works* 3:592 (Sermon 112, §17); modernized and slightly modified
[33] deSilva, *Sacramental Life*, 99.
[34] SeasonsFUSION, https://www.seasonsonline.ca/files/SeasonsFUSION%20Sample.pdf; page 67; accessed January 16, 2019.

EPILOGUE
[1] Cited in Paul W. Chilcote, *Early Methodist Spirituality: Selected Women's Writings* (Nashville: Kingswood Books, 2007), 17.

CPSIA information can be obtained
at www.ICGtesting.com
Printed in the USA
LVHW010206201219
641137LV00009B/55/P